D0931496

Playing Dead

Every 15 Minutes
2002 Program

High School

April 29-30, 2002

Drink and Drive and You're MINE

Playing Dead

Mock Trauma and Folk Drama in Staged High School Drunk-Driving Tragedies

Montana Miller

Volume 2
Ritual, Festival, and Celebration
A series edited by
Jack Santino

UTAH STATE UNIVERSITY PRESS
❖
LOGAN

© 2012 by the University Press of Colorado

Published by Utah State University Press
An imprint of the University Press of Colorado
5589 Arapahoe Avenue, Suite 206C
Boulder, Colorado 80303

The University Press of Colorado is a proud member of

The Association of American University Presses.

AAUP 1937 2012

The University Press of Colorado is a cooperative publishing enterprise supported, in part, by
Adams State University, Colorado State University, Fort Lewis College, Metropolitan State
University of Denver, Regis University, University of Colorado, University of Northern Colorado,
Utah State University, and Western State Colorado University.

ISBN: 978-0-87421-891-6 (cloth)
ISBN: 978-0-87421-892-3 (e-book)

Library of Congress Cataloging-in-Publication Data

Miller, Montana.
    Playing dead : mock trauma and folk drama in staged high school drunk-driving tragedies /
Montana Miller.
        p. cm. — (Ritual, festival, and celebration vol. 2)
    Includes bibliographical references and index.
    ISBN 978-0-87421-891-6 (cloth) — ISBN 978-0-87421-892-3 (e-book)
    1. Folklore—Performance. 2. Folk drama. 3. High school students—Psychology. 4. Death—
Social aspects. I. Title.
    GR72.3.M55 2012
    398.27'7—dc23
                                        2012035279

For *Michael Owen Jones*, who taught me to listen . . .

Jack Santino, whose belief in me lent strength and hope . . .

and *Kathleen Cushman*, who amid the drama
always managed to keep this book's heartbeat alive.

Contents

Foreword

Jack Santino, Series Editor

With *Playing Dead*, Montana Miller has provided a study of a unique phenomenon: the imaginary deaths of high school students, theatricalized with a combination of verisimilitude and fantasy. Teenage death resulting from drunk driving is dramatized in a program called Every 15 Minutes Someone Dies, developed for high schools throughout the United States. In these programs, some students are chosen in advance to play the victims of car fatalities. The "deaths" are announced to the students as if real; police and emergency workers appear at the school as the unfortunate "victim" is retrieved from the wreckage, staged near or on school grounds, and even lifted by helicopter in an emergency life flight. Meanwhile, throughout the day, the Grim Reaper himself wanders the halls of the school building, seizing preselected students every fifteen minutes. Once taken by the figure of Death, these students absent themselves for the rest of the day, as they are now symbolically dead.

There is much more involved in these events, of course, as Montana Miller shows throughout her ethnographic exploration of this unusual program. As scholars, we may be perplexed by such hybrid performances. They do not fit easily into any neat category or genre. Miller sees them primarily as a kind of folk drama, intended to edify and teach. Others may see them as a kind of ritual, because they are fictive, scripted, stylized, and employ traditional symbolism. However, the category "ritual" is not entirely adequate, because the didactic drunk-driving morality plays Miller investigates lack a certain transcendence that marks those sacred ceremonies we widely recognize as rituals.

Playing Dead is a study of precisely the kind of hybrid, porous, symbolic events that I refer to as "ritualesque." I see this ritualesque dimension in a number of contemporary public events, from political rallies to protest demonstrations, from historical memorials to public commemorations of death. As in formal, ceremonial ritual, the intention of the participants is to cause a change in the way things are—to change one's attitudes, to change one's lifestyle, to change one's opinions. As in ritual, the event is largely symbolic in nature but instrumental in intention. Ritual—real ritual—changes things. In its own terms: a wedding joins two people together, a bar mitzvah transforms a boy into a man, an inauguration makes a citizen a president. Some rituals do not have a guaranteed outcome, such as a healing service or votive supplications for favors. But the intention of the actors in performing these rites is to effect a change, a transformation of some aspect of their lives, their surroundings, their world. Other events share many of these characteristics, but are looser, more open ended, less clearly ceremonial. Public protest demonstrations, for instance, feature the prominent display of symbols such as flags and effigies and often feature dramatic performative enactments, music, special costume, and so forth. These are also the motifs of festival, but unlike festival per se, such events have a purpose beyond their immediate enactment: they are intended to change some aspect of the world permanently. They are meant to have effects beyond themselves, in the everyday life of things. One might not see Every 15 Minutes as a fully developed ritual—most likely its participants would not—but it is a symbolic dramatic enactment intended to cause young people to think twice and drive responsibly, to change their behavior.

I believe the study of ritual, festival, and celebration is expanded by the study of these kinds of events and by a consideration of the ritualesque. Mikhail Bakhtin has famously given us the concept of the "carnivalesque," which addresses the inversive, often grotesque ludic elements of festivals such as the medieval Feast of Fools. We can see that the carnivalesque and the ritualesque often coexist; indeed, the attempt to change society is very often accomplished through the performance of carnivalesque extremes and exaggerations.

Playing Dead is an important volume in this series, one that indicates the range of subjects and the theoretical contributions we hope to present in future volumes.

Playing Dead

Alliance City Schools
Presents:

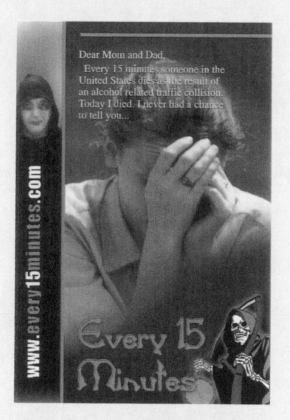

Dear Mom and Dad,
  Every 15 minutes someone in the
United States dies as the result of
an alcohol related traffic collision.
Today I died. I never had a chance
to tell you...

www.every15minutes.com

Every 15 Minutes

May 9 & 10, 2002

1

Every 15 Minutes Someone Dies

As the first class period begins at a local high school, tragic events—prepared through months of careful planning—begin to unfold. Over the next hours the "Grim Reaper," cloaked in black and carrying a scythe, will roam the hallways, pulling students from classrooms at fifteen-minute intervals to represent "one person killed every fifteen minutes by a drunk-driving accident." Each victim's eulogy will be read aloud by a police deputy, as classmates listen in stunned silence. Later, the twenty "Living Dead" will return to their classes, bearing white face paint and coroner's tags, and they will remain silent for the rest of the day. Their obituaries are posted in the school foyer, their gravestones are erected in the courtyard, and their parents receive realistic "death notifications" at homes and workplaces. In the midst of it all, local emergency services personnel will simulate a fatal car accident in the school parking lot; students play the roles of drunk drivers and casualties, "bleeding" with gory makeup. A 911 call is broadcast over the public address system, and sirens wail as fire trucks, ambulances, and hearses respond to the scene.

This is only the first act of an elaborate two-day event commonly known as "Every 15 Minutes" in which tragedy is staged in an effort to transform and inculcate values in high school students. As a drunk-driving-prevention tactic, the program has spread with astonishing momentum since the early 1990s; but it is not nationally organized or sponsored, and it has neither a precise origin nor one "official" version. Replicated and modified in hundreds of communities around the country, Every 15 Minutes—often called "E15M" for short—is collaboratively produced by schools, law enforcement, and community volunteers. Local versions share similar sequences and themes, symbolic actions and imagery. Participants, through firsthand interaction and personal communication with colleagues and friends in other towns, pass on the word about E15M.

As Every 15 Minutes has spread across the country in hundreds of local versions of the program, I have documented dozens of examples—firsthand and through archived documents and videos of the program—each building on a consistent structure and multiple themes. These events feature common and varying elements of costuming, role-playing, music, slogans, poetry, publicity, posters, props, rhetoric, and emotional display.

What is it that schools are producing here? Documentary or soap opera? I have come to understand this contemporary American tradition in the terms of its enactors, who, as they explained their aesthetic and logistical choices to me, repeatedly asserted, "It's a *drama!*" The production of Every 15 Minutes stages tragedy as "realistically" as possible at the same time as it captures participants' imagination and attention with the dramatic elements of costuming and playacting. The event constantly juxtaposes the presentational and the representational; that is, reality and fantasy intertwine and merge (Pettit 1997).

In this book, I examine the complex interplay of realistic and unrealistic elements in Every 15 Minutes, and the ways participants play with these ambiguous frames throughout the event. This phenomenon illuminates a great deal about the moral messages conveyed, displayed, and debated when education and folklore meet and merge.

In Every 15 Minutes, especially during climactic moments, many role-players and spectators weep—on cue, spontaneously, or somewhere in between. In the standard scenario, one student role-player is rushed from the crash scene to the hospital, where she flatlines and dies in the presence of her parents (who exhibit reactions of despair and hysteria, though aware it is a simulation). The Living Dead are secluded overnight at a remote location. Seated at tables stocked with boxes of Kleenex, they must write letters to their parents "from the grave." The next day, at the mock funeral and assembly (ostensibly the cathartic moment of the program), students are reunited with their families and they read their letters in public, often breaking into tears.

Enormous resources of time, money, energy, and emotion go into this dramatic reenactment. It includes months of planning, full-scale EMS operations, helicopter evacuations for critically injured "victims," tours of prisons, courthouses, and morgues, and video crews documenting the action. Participants describing the program attribute great importance to following the planned scenario; they devote hours of meetings to hashing out the details of the script, the graphic detail of the images, the rules to be followed by those "playing" in the drama, and decisions about which students get to play key roles.

However, during the actual two-day event, things rarely go according to plan. Even those who are most invested in the play (including school administrators and law-enforcement officials) frequently deviate from the script or the rules. Accidents, oversights, improvisations, subversions, and deliberate sabotage constantly interrupt the smooth progression of events. Despite all this, in the end, organizers consistently judge the play a hit. But the range of responses to the performance is wider than administrators acknowledge; while many students participate in the simulated grieving, others express skepticism, outrage, indifference, or amusement.

Every 15 Minutes, as an emerging tradition, involves many symbolic elements, from its shared beliefs (for example, "Teenagers think they are immortal") to its evocative slogans. The program's catchy title, based on a 1980s statistic, persists despite improvements in the numbers. Organizers told me that a current and more accurate statistic (by the late 1990s, the number had dropped to one death every thirty-three minutes; by 2008, it was one every forty-five minutes) "wouldn't hit home the same way" that the number fifteen did.

PLAYING DEAD: WHY AND HOW?

This book is based on my observations of the Every 15 Minutes program, a folk drama or play in which participants are continually shifting frames. (That is, their actions are interpreted—by themselves and by others—in constantly changing ways.) I explore the key aspects of this emergent tradition, paying particular attention to its unplanned elements. While many may wonder whether E15M actually makes any difference—whether it "works" to prevent drunk driving—I do not aim to answer this elusive question. From a cultural standpoint, the more crucial questions involve *why* people create and re-create these mock tragedies.

- How do people modify and personalize the drama, and the rules of the play, to fit their local contexts?
- In what ways (planned and unplanned) do participants mark out, and shift between, frames during the play? How do they manipulate and improvise on the rules or script?

- How may such frame shifting and rule breaking affect participants' engagement in, and perception of, the drama? What elements of E15M are essential, remaining stable as the program
  is transmitted over time and space?
- What constitutes E15M's continued appeal and perceived success, even when things do not go according to plan?

This book is grounded in the scholarly concepts of folk drama and
play; it will explore the spontaneous nature of what is often assumed to be
prescribed ritual in these forms of folklore. I use ethnographic methods to
reveal the perspectives of participants in events that entail shifting frames,
as well as ambiguous and dark aspects of play. *Playing Dead* challenges some
assumptions that previous scholars have made about the process of engagement or engrossment in folk dramas and the implications of that process for
the "success" and perpetuation of such traditions.

Folklorists have used the concept of folk (community-based) drama to
trace variation in a tradition, often analyzing folk drama in the context of
its surrounding culture. Usually these studies have focused on the anatomy
of the drama, cataloguing examples without delving into the varied experiences of participants. Many scholars of play have made similar general-
izations about human experience, looking at games or dramas as reflective
of culture or as functional in psychological development. Some scholars of
play, however, have paid more attention to individuals as active agents with
strategies and motivations. Play-frame analysis has enabled some to explore
the complexities of play, in which distinctions between reality and fiction
are frequently blurred.

Frame analysis helps scholars to examine how participants in dramas
like E15M cross the lines between audience and performer. Certain markers intentionally set E15M apart from everyday life, in its own specialized
time and place; these markers may be theatrical cues—including costume,
makeup, music, and gesture—or verbal references to the event. Presenters,
as they communicate utilitarian messages, consistently step in and out of
the performative or "make-believe" (Goffman 1974) frame; they blur the
distinction between performer and audience, earnestly proclaiming the
importance of the very drama they enact. The event also blurs representation and reality, combining presentation of realistic images (the simulated
car wreck) with representation of supernatural ones (the Grim Reaper, the
Living Dead). While some folklorists have contended that folk drama does

not require participants to *believe* in either aspect, some have argued that it *does* require the collaboration of players and spectators, who together sustain the fantasy by choosing to behave as though the fictional events depicted were real (Ellis 1981; Pettit 1997).

These ideas of collaboration and engagement, discussed by various scholars of play and folk drama, need further development. To address this issue, I illustrate here a range of responses and perceptions to a production that is intended to sweep up everyone into a shared frame of staged tragedy. One organizer explained to me, "We do so *much* of the imagery . . . the motorcycles, the fire engines, the emergency vehicles, the hearse from the funeral home. And because it's all so *vivid,* it really catches their attention and at that point, they're caught up in the drama." The reactions I witnessed and documented at various field sites, among teenagers and adults alike, were far more varied than this organizer's assessment suggests.

In addition, my fieldwork revealed an aspect of Every 15 Minutes that typical promotions of the program do not include: it can be fun. As one school employee remarked, "The community loves it, and so do the police officers and the fire [department workers] and so on, because they usually do a drill anyway, and for them this is more fun." Another teacher attested to the appeal of the program's "sensationalism," explaining: "Kids are fighting to be in the body bags. They want to be the one in the limelight." In the staging of the tragic scene, fun is not explicitly planned or officially sanctioned. But apparently, there is something fun about all this drama— the dressing up, the graphic makeup, the sirens, the excitement and tears, the emotional music. The influential psychologist Mihaly Csikszentmihaly (1975) has argued that fun cannot always be dissected and analyzed. Even so, we must not discount the appeal and excitement of a folkloric event officially described as serious and traumatic. Furthermore, participants may use Every 15 Minutes as an occasion for expression that would normally be inhibited; during this extraordinary event, everyday order is suspended, and many can voice feelings and show emotion in the safety of reassurances that it's all just pretend.

Finally, innumerable factors affect the ubiquitous frame shifting and rule breaking in E15M as well as in other allegedly educational or preventive programs whose symbolic importance their promoters tout so highly. Many of these factors are idiosyncratic and spontaneous, depending more on individual personalities, interactions, and accidents than on predictable cause and effect. Still, patterns do emerge in the ways people bend and break the rules, and these patterns can reveal valuable insights into the human element in folklore. During my research, I had the chance to observe many of these human elements shaping the enactment of the "tragedy."

Between 1999 and 2003, I investigated Every 15 Minutes intensively, both by attending events in person and by examining videos and other artifacts and records of the program. I tracked examples down in dozens of states across the country, each event a variation on a consistent structure and themes. Ultimately, I compiled a database that included hundreds of local versions of the program, from a California suburban school of thousands to a tiny rural school in Maine. I watched the staged tragedy unfold at urban high schools in Los Angeles, wealthy suburban high schools in Maryland, and a small rural school in New Mexico. During in-depth interviews, dozens of local sponsors and administrators—E15M's "tradition-bearers," to borrow folklorist Carl von Sydow's term for those who participate in the passing on of a specific tradition (1965)—explained to me how they learned about the program through their professional networks and why they perceive it to be such a powerful collective experience.

Everywhere, it seems, E15M's combination of realistic and fantastic imagery works to striking dramatic effect. And as the tradition has taken hold and continues to spread, I have noticed E15M exemplifying a trend in educational settings: communities across the country stage various gruesome dramas, from lockdown drills to haunted houses, aimed especially at transforming teenagers' attitudes and behavior. My descriptive study provides insight not only in the field of folklore but also in related disciplines such as education, anthropology, sociology, psychology, and public health. Historically, folkloristic studies of similar presentational and representational events have been classified variously as folk drama or as play; scholars in both of these areas have provided grounding concepts for my research, helping me to observe and interpret what happens "Every 15 Minutes."

WHAT IS FOLK DRAMA?

According to Thomas Pettit, writing in the 1997 encyclopedia *Folklore*, folk drama is distinct from theatrical performance in that it is characteristically presentational, rather than fully representational: "While consciously representing something other than themselves and the time and place of performance, performers remain conscious of themselves as presenting a show to an audience in a given time and place. Dramatic illusion, although aimed for or gestured at, is therefore breached consistently by awareness of context and relationship to the audience . . . by direct address from within the fiction of the play world to the audience or even interaction (verbal and/ or physical) with spectators" (212).

Most studies of folk drama have examined discontinued traditions of the past (such as Christmas mumming and medieval passion plays) or have been limited to religious contexts. While local folk dramas that reenact historical events, parody weddings, accompany political protests, or thrive as camp skits exist (Ellis 1981; Mechling 1980; Pettit 1997; Taft 1996), in-depth studies of such living examples are rare. Sylvia Rodriguez's *The Matachines Dance* (1996) is one exception; the author describes a current southwestern dance/drama, symbolic of interethnic conflict, emerging from a common tradition. Rodriguez relates variants of the performance to their broader community contexts, but she does not attempt to bring forth the voices and experiences of the participants, as I do. The spectacle of professional wrestling has attracted scholars' notice as well (Campbell 1996; Dawson 1992; Rickard 1999; Saunders 1998), yet this form of popular entertainment lacks the local variation and intimacy between actors and audience that has been said to typically define folk drama (Green 1978). In wrestling, professional players travel from venue to venue; in Every 15 Minutes, in contrast, members of the community act as players in each local version.

Folk drama thrives in numerous examples in educational or youth-oriented settings (Taft 1996), from Christmas pageants to church-sponsored Halloween Hell Houses (Gordon 1999; Katz 1998; Ratliff 2002a; Squires 1998; Verhovek 1996), but scholars have rarely noticed these traditions and have paid even less attention to eliciting their participants' points of view. Studies that consider folk drama in education, like studies of ritual performances in general, have primarily focused on the nonsecular context (Kapferer 1981; Lesko 1988), and typically have not emphasized the creative variation and subservience to context that, as Pettit (1997) notes, characterize folk drama as a genre.

Bill Ellis (1981) has described a staged summer camp ritual in which encounters with "supernatural" characters create a sense of unity among campers of diverse backgrounds. Ellis writes that folk drama requires participants' willingness to *act as though they believe* in its fictional elements and characters. He contends that a successful folk drama depends upon the willing collaboration of its participants—players and spectators—in this temporary unreality; those apparently caught up in the drama behave as though it were real while implicitly understanding it as fiction. The issue of engagement, though, has not caught the attention of most writers who document and compare versions of a folk drama, even when they describe the performance as a political or educational tool.

Every 15 Minutes, as I will illustrate, clearly represents an example of folk drama, an often neglected genre of folklore. Just as Pettit (1997) writes that "more or less accurate impersonation exists alongside figures from the fauna of local myth and fantasy," (211) E15M's combination of realistic and fantastic imagery works to striking dramatic effect. Emergency services arrive at the crash scene with sirens, flares, helicopters, "the Jaws of Life," breathalyzer tests, and body bags; hospitals simulate resuscitation attempts; guest speakers recount personal tragedies; funeral directors give guided tours; paramedics tell their worst stories with tears in their eyes. Yet it is the Grim Reaper who oversees a dozen sweating firefighters as they pry the top off a crushed vehicle, as an officer administers sobriety tests to a swaying "drunk driver," and as the loudspeaker broadcasts students' hypothetical obituaries. Through the entire scene, this huge figure cloaked in black and carrying a plastic scythe wanders silently, while the sight of their classmates made up with chalky face paint and black raccoon eyes reduces some teenagers to tears.

The combination of real and fantasy also highlights the multiple frames through which one may perceive the scene. Theories of play, including play-frame analysis, will therefore prove equally useful in grounding my study.

THE STUDY OF PLAY

Early on in the history of folkloristics, William Newell compiled a collection, *Games and Songs of American Children* (1883), in which he catalogued and described the characteristics and "rules" of play, focusing exclusively on children as the population engaging in such activity. Robert Georges, in his essay "The Relevance of Models for Analyses of Traditional Play Activities" (1969), laments the fact that most folkloristic study of play has been confined to comparative collections of children's games; he cites such examples as Beckwith (1922); Brewster (1952); Cox (1942); and Thyregod (1931). Georges calls for a deeper understanding of traditional play activities, beyond the survivalist, diffusionist, and structuralist (Dundes 1964) approaches taken by previous folklore scholars; in order to understand the phenomenon as a whole, individual examples must be studied holistically, from the participants' point of view.

Play as a serious topic of study has been largely influenced by the writing of linguist Johan Huizinga, whose *Homo Ludens: A Study of the Play Element in Culture* appeared in 1950. In this book, Huizinga describes play as a process that involves "stepping out of 'real' life into a temporary sphere of activity with a disposition all its own," but that works by "absorbing the player intensely and utterly" and proceeds "according to fixed rules and in an orderly manner." He notes that play is "'played out' within certain limits of time and space. It contains its own course and meanings" (9). While Huizinga conceptualizes play as having fluid boundaries, he sees it as a realm where devoted players follow agreed-upon rules.

Most studies of play have treated the phenomenon as a survival from more primitive states of development (Newell 1963 [1883]; Opie and Opie 1959, 1969), as a function of psychological development in children (Erikson 1963; Piaget 1962), or as a reflection of culture, as in Clifford Geertz's "Deep Play: Notes on the Balinese Cockfight" (1972). Other scholars of play have included Roger Caillois, who in his 1961 book *Man, Play and Games* emphasizes the element of chance in play rather than its competitive aspects and addresses the potential for spontaneity and improvisation in some types of play, and Roberts, Arth, and Bush, who focus on defining the nature of games in their essay "Games in Culture" (1959). Simulations and role-playing games, whether physical or in cyberspace, have drawn increasing attention in recent years, as scholars have examined the relationship of play to reality (Fine 1983; Holcomb 2000; McCarthy 1990; McGonigal 2003). Csikszentmihalyi, in *Beyond Boredom and Anxiety: The Experience of Play in Work and Games* (1975), points out the nature of play as enjoyment and fun for its own sake; still, Brian Sutton-Smith (a prolific author on the subject of play and games) writes with Diana Kelly-Byrne in *The Masks of Play* that this aspect of play calls for more attention (1984). These scholars, along with Richard Schechner (1988, 1993), have developed the notion of "dark play," suggesting that adults and children alike may use play as a setting to mask behavior unacceptable in ordinary life.

Play-frame analysis, in the tradition of scholars of play including Gregory Bateson, Brian Sutton-Smith, and Jay Mechling, contributes to the understanding of any complex performance in which participants are constantly stepping back and forth between reality and fantasy. Scholars have considered the "real-life" mode to be marked by the expectation of "serious" activity in everyday life (Goffman 1974; Schechner 1988).

Bateson (1972) and Handelman (1977) have advanced a theory of meta-communicational frames, proposing that the frame of everyday life carries a meta-message that grounds people in physical space and time, and holds them accountable for their physical and verbal actions and for their social commitments. Special, set-apart play activities thus exist in separate frames with different meta-messages; identifying the markers that distinguish these frames is the researcher's challenge. Frames are continually shifting, creating what Sutton-Smith calls "the ambiguity of play" (1997).

Those who have studied play and games have often noted the differences between plans and actual enactments as players strategize, compete, improvise, and deviate from the prescribed rules. With few exceptions, though (including Suchman 1987), these analyses have limited themselves to children's game play and to understanding how it is transformed in practice. Anthropologist Marjorie Goodwin, in her study of girls' hopscotch, points out that "a major problem of research on games has been that much research has concentrated on the *forms* of games . . . rather than the interaction through which a game is accomplished *in situ*" (1995, 262). Goodwin and others (Fine 1986; Goldstein 1971; Hughes 1991) have argued that scholars need to examine how children's games are interpreted and transformed in play, focusing on how participants "actively collaborate in constructing the game of the moment" (Goodwin 1995, 262).

Studies of play have generally confined themselves to the games and make-believe activities of children (Georges 1969), though some have developed "game theory" models and applied them to adults' gambling and sometimes political or economic behaviors. Few have considered contexts in which adults and children collaborate and act as strategists in a play scenario such as the one acted out in the Every 15 Minutes drama. By contributing in this way to the literature on play, this book seeks to add to a historically neglected genre in folklore studies.

APPROACHING THE SCENE

In conducting my fieldwork for this book, I adopted an ethnographic approach that included naturalistic observation, formal and informal interviews, and archival research. My qualitative study of Every 15 Minutes employs the concepts of folk drama and play in a descriptive and comparative analysis based on the events I attended and documented in a diverse range of communities. The data I gathered incorporate multiple types of information and points of view, and I base much of my analysis on the expressed perspectives of E15M participants.

At schools in California, New Mexico, and Maryland, I tape-recorded hours of interviews (both formal and informal) with students, teachers, administrators, law-enforcement personnel, paramedics, counselors, parents, and anyone else who was willing to talk to me. My interviews were in depth and open ended (Spradley 1979), eliciting participants' views of the many symbolic and dramatic aspects of E15M. I addressed topics such as decision making in planning and presentation; which images they found most powerful; how much graphic detail they thought necessary, how much was "too much," and why; and how they assessed the program's outcome. Many of these interviewees were the participants most invested in the construction and performance of the program; but as I observed the enactment of the two-day event firsthand, I also witnessed the reactions of the student body at large, including those who mocked, ignored, or disrupted the proceedings. I attended the "Living Dead" activities, accompanying groups on tours of prisons and courthouses, sitting in on their retreats, and in some cases witnessing simulated flatlining scenes at the hospital. I recorded my observations with a laptop computer, notebook, or tape recorder, depending on which technique was most practical and least intrusive in a given situation.

Supplementing a wealth of archival information (from media accounts; from Internet sites; and from videos, planning, and presentational material provided to me by communities around the country), my fieldwork allowed me glimpses of how Every 15 Minutes *really* happens. How did adults and teens take advantage of the opportunity to "play" with or against each other, and adapt generic rules to their own relationships? I was struck by the ubiquitous unplanned elements and how they might affect the "success" of the play; thus, in this book I explore discrepancies between the plans—carefully laid over months of preparations—and the actual events as they were performed over the two days of drama. I describe various kinds of spontaneity, improvisation, and deviation from the script in the examples of E15M I witnessed.

I observed some participants weeping and fawning over their "dead"; some looking on, amused but attentive; some willing to participate if they got their chance to deliver a speech; some freezing in the spotlight; and some compelled to interrupt the eulogizing and hog the pulpit. As I found that key personalities and relationships often complicated or derailed the smooth performance of the drama, I considered it important to ask people about what contextual factors they saw affecting the process and perception of the event. For example, in one community where it was commonly known that the woman running the program always had to have things "her way," rules could change constantly at her whim without the loss of other players' collaboration and consent. But at another site, the committee that had spent months planning every detail felt betrayed when the school principal interrupted the "reaping" process to call the entire senior class to a meeting at which he announced his impending departure for a job in a different district. "I can't believe he did that—why did he pick today of all days? Nine months of work down the drain!" complained one of the community resource officers. Sometimes the breaks in the frame are unintentional and uncontrollable; sometimes they are deliberate and creative. Among organizers, the rules that govern symbolic image and action may be explained in reverential tones, but during the emergent enactment of the program, they seem to be easily broken, disagreed on, subverted, forgotten, or simply abandoned.

By talking to as many people as possible over an extended period of fieldwork, I collected a breadth and depth of ethnographic information that has enabled me to discern and reflect upon emerging patterns. Techniques of open coding and narrative analysis (Emerson, Fretz, and Shaw 1995) have helped me to identify and interpret these patterns.

My fieldwork reveals many aspects of how people actually participate, and do not participate, in E15M, and how their behaviors differ from official and promotional descriptions. Yet the program persists and remains tremendously appealing to organizers, even when many aspects do not go as planned. The fact that such unplanned elements do not seem to destroy the play is important for those who study forms of play, ritual, and drama— and it has particular relevance for those who organize or study such events in America's schools, where they grow increasingly popular. For example, a Doctors of Death drama followed a similar scenario to E15M, but with three students costumed as doctors wheeling gurneys down the hallways and pulling students from class to represent those killed by drug abuse (Reber 2001). Schools also stage lockdown drills to prepare for terrorist attacks or school shootings. What accounts for the appeal of such gruesome reenactment and tragic role-play? Possible explanations include opportunities for creative expression and dark play, for a controlled experience of death and loss, for a break from the everyday monotony of schooling, for community and family bonding, for the chance to be the center of attention, and for the pure *fun* of it all.

The evidence I gathered, especially during moments when rules and frames were shifting or broken by participants, will help to further develop the theories considered in this book, challenging scholars' assumptions about what determines the "success" or "failure" of play or folk drama. Scholars dealing with the phenomenon that sociologist Erving Goffman (1974) termed "engrossment" have emphasized the willing collaboration of all participants (including spectators) in the scenario. However, I have observed many instances of collaboration going awry without derailing the entire event. And, contrary to common assumptions in educational institutional contexts, the people who break the rules or cause glitches in the proceedings are as often adults as they are students.

Ethnographic methods, which bring out a range of perspectives and experiences through the voices of informants, can reveal diverse and dissenting opinions that tend to be silenced in the dominant discourse. In studying a folk drama event where individuals' experiences may be overlooked, and an educational program in which administrators' perspectives can drown out those of students, ethnographic methods are especially appropriate (Erickson 1984; Farrell 1988; Varenne and McDermott 1998). My study reveals human processes that shape enactments of prescribed programs, and the potential contributions—creative as well as problematic—of that human element.

WHAT LIES HEREAFTER

Chapter 2, "Backdrop for the Scene," provides a backdrop for Every 15 Minutes and its dramatic scenes. This overview incorporates a discussion of the drunk-driving issue in American history and culture, as well as the history of awareness and activism regarding the problem. I present various prevention approaches that educators and lawmakers have taken, and general perceptions as to the effectiveness of such approaches. I describe a range of prevention efforts—predecessors to E15M—based on experiential learning and scare tactics. The chapter then chronicles the history of the program itself, providing an overview of its anatomy, its theatrical elements, and its typical structure. I highlight the variations that have developed as E15M's popularity as a drunk-driving-prevention program has spread, and discuss the program's transmission, stability, and change over time and space.

Chapter 3, "Marked for Death: Ambiguity and Slippery Steps in Frames of Play," analyzes Every 15 Minutes as a form of play in which participants shift frames continually. In various planned and unplanned ways, rules and frames are used, changed, and broken by participants. Identifying various markers that frame the event and the rules of conduct within it, I discuss the ambiguity and fluidity of these boundaries and these frames of "real" and "pretend."

Chapter 4, "Engrossed Out: Every 15 Minutes as Folk Drama," presents E15M as a dynamic form of folk drama that combines presentation and representation, particularly addressing issues of engagement or willing collaboration in the drama. I present and discuss participants' perceptions of whether, and why, the program "works." My interpretation of the data collected during my fieldwork challenges some scholarly ideas about the necessity of engrossment for folk drama to succeed.

In Chapter 5, "The Dazzle and Darkness of Play," I examine the growing appeal of this new form of folk drama, analyzing its public memorialization of the "dead" and its opportunities for people to engage in dark play. Exploring and expanding on this idea, I present examples that illustrate the appeal of dark play, emphasizing the ambiguity and variety of people's individual experiences. A range of related forms of dramatic dark play is growing in popularity in contemporary America.

In Chapter 6, "Shattering Frames: The Crash through YouTube's Window," I will explain how the explosion of YouTube and youth-generated videos influenced the spread and evolution of the Every 15 Minutes drama, adding new dimensions and new technological conduits for discourse, performance, and play.

The themes addressed in this book, and the phenomena described and interpreted here, call for more attention in academia and beyond. They carry implications for the future study of drama and play, for American educational culture, and for the folk culture of America itself.

2

Backdrop for the Scene

We have a doctor who is incredible—he did it the first year, and he loved it so much he's doing it with us ever since . . . He comes out and visits with the family in the waiting room to tell them all the injuries, and he goes into great detail, and he has the parents in tears— knowing that it's not true, but he's so real—he tells them all that, and then they take them into the room and they just talk to the child and it happens then. They watch the child die.

—Every 15 Minutes organizer

DRUNK DRIVING IN AMERICA

THE STAGED TRAGEDY OF EVERY 15 MINUTES TAKES place against a backdrop of real carnage on American highways. Drunk-driving fatalities, as well as public concern about the problem, have been tracked over the years by various government, academic, and advocacy groups.

Alarming statistics are easy to find; in fact, the quantity and range of sources of information can be daunting. Countless websites trumpet the "cold, hard, sobering facts" (as AlcoholAlert.com puts it) about the deadly toll drunk driving takes. However, with new studies coming out regularly from a variety of reputable organizations, statistics are confounding and do not necessarily correspond to the rhetoric commonly used in anti-drunk-driving efforts. For example, according to the Centers for Disease Control's 2008 data, available at http://www.cdc.gov, alcohol-related motor-vehicle crashes kill someone approximately every forty-five (not fifteen) minutes, although a nonfatal injury does occur every two minutes.

The National Highway Traffic Safety Administration (NHTSA) defines a fatal traffic crash as "alcohol-related" if either a driver or a non-occupant (for example, a pedestrian) had a blood alcohol concentration

DOI:10.7330/9780874218923.c02   15

(BAC) of 0.01 grams per deciliter or greater in a police-reported traffic crash. According to laws in most states, persons with a BAC of 0.08 or higher are considered to be "intoxicated" or "alcohol-impaired" (NHTSA 2008a). (The number of alcohol-related fatalities in the United States in 2008 was 13,846; alcohol-*impaired* fatalities, with BAC of .08 or greater, numbered 11,773.)

Government research has consistently shown that young drivers are more often involved in alcohol-related crashes than any other comparable age group. A 2009 publication from the Centers for Disease Control (CDC) reported that "at all levels of blood alcohol concentration (BAC), the risk of involvement in a motor-vehicle crash is greater for teens than for older drivers." In 2008, it said, fully one quarter of drivers aged fifteen to twenty who died in crashes were intoxicated. And 10 percent of teenagers said that in the preceding month they had driven after drinking alcohol (CDC 2009).

The NHTSA also released statistics on male drivers between fifteen and twenty years of age who were involved in fatal crashes in 2005. Among these drivers, 26 percent had been drinking (NHTSA 2008b). Numerous sources of state and federal government data show that alcohol-crash involvement rates, share of the alcohol-crash problem, and alcohol-crash risk all reach their highest points with young drivers.

Yet in contrast to the rhetoric of the Every 15 Minutes program, trends in drunk-driving statistics have shown steady improvement over the years. The NHTSA has been tracking the percentage of fatal crashes that involved intoxicated drivers over the years, and notes a significant and steady decline in this percentage between 1982 and 2005, from 35 percent to 20 percent. It attributes this decline to various factors, but particularly credits tougher legislation and changes in demographics (e.g., higher average driver age, more female drivers, and lower alcohol consumption per capita) (NHTSA 2008a).

Already in 2001 (when Every 15 Minutes had arrived as a common and acclaimed intervention in high schools across the United States) the NHTSA was reporting that measures of fatalities in alcohol-related crashes had "declined markedly since objective data on the problem became available." The fatality *rate* (which accounts for population growth) had declined nearly 50 percent since 1982, according to those data. "Clearly, alcohol-related fatal crashes are a much smaller societal problem at the millennium than they were 20, or even 10, years ago," the NHTSA concluded. Since blood alcohol concentration was not routinely measured in nonfatal crashes, it was not clear whether those rates had decreased as well (NHTSA 2001).

At this point, the number of young people who died in crashes in which an intoxicated young driver was involved had declined by almost 63 percent, according to the CDC's Vital Statistics Mortality Data (2003). Drinking and driving was no longer the leading cause of death for teenagers.

By 2009, even more dramatic improvement was revealed by the Insurance Institute for Highway Safety's Highway Loss Data Institute, whose "fatality facts" about teenagers estimated that the percentage of fatally injured drunk drivers sixteen to seventeen years old was 14 percent—down 65 percent from 1982. (As noted earlier, most of this decline occurred in the 1980s.) Fatally injured drivers in older age groups showed significantly less decline in their rates of alcohol involvement (IIHS 2009).

The NHTSA's 2008 report acknowledged the efforts of activist groups and programs such as Mothers against Drunk Driving (MADD) and Students against Destructive Decisions (SADD), but stated that determining the impact of such efforts on fatality reductions was not feasible. It noted the lack of reliable information quantifying these programs and their efforts, and suggested that the real difference came about because of the stricter laws that activist groups publicized (NHTSA 2008b).

Widespread belief, however, is unmoved by the government data showing improvement in alcohol-related death statistics. During the course of my fieldwork I observed educators, drunk-driving-prevention advocates, and often journalists who were concerned less with accuracy than with communicating to teenagers the most "impactful" statements possible. For example, the day after Every 15 Minutes was held at one Maryland school, the *Washington Post* account of it stated that "such events have been on the rise across the country for the past few decades as the number of teenagers involved in drunken driving accidents has been increasing"

(Hedgpeth 2001). Local television coverage of E15M frequently cites drunk driving as the leading killer of teenagers, along with the obsolete "every 15 minutes" statistic.

Although most Every 15 Minutes organizers prefer to emphasize alarming statistics when speaking to students—even if it means using outdated or inaccurate figures—some do acknowledge the declining fatality rates, and they frequently comment that this improvement has occurred thanks to programs like E15M. However, national research organizations (such as the Insurance Institute for Highway Safety and the Highway Loss Data Institute, which post a comprehensive review of the latest research at http:// www.iihs.org) have credited stricter laws and more aggressive law enforcement, not educational prevention efforts, for the change. To reduce alcohol-related fatal crashes among youth, all states have adopted a minimum legal drinking age (MLDA) of twenty-one as well as zero tolerance laws setting a BAC limit of .02 or lower for drivers under the age of twenty-one. The NHTSA has long supported such laws; early on, it concluded that states adopting MLDAs of twenty-one in the early 1980s documented a 10 to 15 percent decline in alcohol-related traffic deaths among drivers in the targeted ages compared with states that did not adopt such laws. In its 2008 report, the NHTSA noted that this progress leveled off after 1997, but that these laws had remained effective in reducing the problem (2008b).

Almost all states and the District of Columbia now require that their young novice drivers pass through a graduated driver licensing system, a three-step licensing process that gradually phases in the licensing privilege as new skills are learned. These systems may include such features as nighttime driving restrictions, certified hours of parental instruction, zero tolerance for alcohol and drugs, passenger restrictions, and accelerated sanctions for traffic violations (Governors Highway Safety Association and Insurance Institute for Highway Safety 2011).

There is no definitive answer to the question of what has worked, or what could work better, to reduce teenage drunk-driving fatalities. In discussions during Every 15 Minutes events I attended, if anyone brought up the death toll's change for the better, usually someone attributed the progress to E15M and/or programs like it. Law-enforcement personnel were more likely to mention the positive effect of stricter law enforcement and graduated license programs. Participants rarely discussed other possible explanations, such as the particularly relevant issue of improvements in emergency medical technology and training.

HISTORY AND EVALUATION OF
DRUNK-DRIVING PREVENTION

When the first Students against Drunk Driving group was founded by Robert Anastas at a high school in Wayland, Massachusetts, in September 1981, its stated purpose was "to alert and inform high school students across the nation about the potential dangers of the misuse and abuse of alcohol as it relates to driving" (Anastas 1982). This marked the beginning of a period of increased concern in response to a problem that had become epidemic.

The NHTSA stated in its 2001 report "Alcohol and Highway Safety 2001: A Review of the State of Knowledge" that according to research, "experiencing a prior negative event (such as an arrest or a crash) has a positive effect on one's decision to drive after drinking, tending to make a driver less inclined to drive after drinking." Factors that have a negative effect include a lack of knowledge of the impairing effects of alcohol or a misinterpretation of the cues of impairment, a reduction of inhibitions at higher BACs, a lowered perception of alcohol-crash risk, and a neglect of social norms after drinking. Research suggests that it is not just the impairing effects of alcohol that favor a decision to drive after drinking; some drivers plan to drink knowing that they will drive afterward.

Other perspectives on risk prevention contribute to lively debate in the research literature. Some argue that punitive measures have little effect, while physicians' screenings for substance abuse, subsequent counseling, taxes on beer and wine, and enforcement of minimum drinking age laws can decisively reduce drunk driving (Escobedo 1994). The reasoning behind "problem behavior theory" (Klepp, Perry, and Jacobs 1991) suggests that because behaviors easily become entrenched once they begin, school-based, peer-led educational prevention programs are most likely to help if they are designed to reach students before they obtain driver's licenses.

A theory that emerged in the late 1990s, the "social norms strategy of behavior change," has been implemented in several university studies of students' misperceptions as to how much others drink. Colleges across the country have launched publicity campaigns; rather than giving dire warnings to frighten people into healthy behavior, these schools try to create positive peer pressure to conform to more moderate "true norms" of drinking habits (Haines 1998; Jeffrey et al. 2003; Perkins 2002; Stryker 1999). The impact and usefulness of this strategy have been debated among those concerned with prevention. Whether it could have a significant, large-scale effect on drinking and driving behaviors was tested for the first time in a NHTSA-sponsored study released in 2005, titled "Montana's MOST of Us Don't Drink and Drive Campaign: A Social Norms Strategy to Reduce Impaired Driving among 21-to-34-Year-Olds" (Linkenbach and Perkins 2005). Participants in western Montana who were exposed to media messages promoting positive social norms reported a 13.7 percent decrease in drinking and driving, and a 15 percent increase in the use of designated drivers. The study's authors concluded optimistically that media social norms intervention can change attitudes and behaviors; but they acknowledged that their findings could not be confirmed, as they had no data on drunk-driving fatalities or BAC levels to corroborate the self-reports of their subjects. "Self-reported surveys are a reliable and widely-used method of data collection," the authors assert. But self-reported data are notoriously suspect—for example, strong psychosocial influences can reduce but also affect self-reporting of drunk-driving behavior (MacKinnon et al. 1994)—and self-reporting is perhaps even more questionable in the context of a study focused on perceptions of peer culture and fitting in.

Three major approaches to intervention in drinking and driving have dominated the discourse of prevention: the educational approach, the peer approach, and the environmental approach. Educational approaches to alcohol abuse prevention have been found to affect students' knowledge but not their behavior; however, it is possible that education can result in many students being more likely to intervene when they see a peer about to take the wheel after drinking (McKnight 1986). Proponents of these programs often tout their effectiveness based on the chance that they might influence even one student to refrain from drinking and driving.

School and governmental approaches to drug education have tended to mix and match approaches and programs, many of them emphasizing abstinence (conservative administrations increasingly earmarked federal funding for efforts of this type) and others focusing on harm minimization. Researchers have noted, though, that this mixing and matching leaves students with slight exposure to the different methods. Thus the various programs are unlikely to result in consistent behavioral effects over time, and evaluation is problematic (Hawthorne 2001).

A search through the exhaustive archives available on the National Institute on Alcohol Abuse and Alcoholism (NIAAA 2011) Alcohol and Alcohol Problems Science Database turns up a great deal of hypothesizing, but little consensus, on the topic of alcohol abuse in adolescents. Drunk-driving-prevention programs that have come under study tend to fall into the "education" or the "punitive" categories, and while law enforcement and education overlap in examples such as the once ubiquitous (now arguably discredited) DARE program, the results of even those supposedly integrative programs have been questionable. Public discussion of negative results has often been hampered by political investment in the initiative.

As mentioned earlier, self-reporting and self-selection of participants affects the outcome of traditional evaluation studies. And, not surprisingly, researchers who have studied peer-to-peer programs such as SADD have found that those involved perceived the programs to be helpful (Leaf and Preusser 1995). Gender differences may be substantial: researchers have found girls more likely to participate in anti-drug programs (Woodman 1994), and boys twice as likely to be involved in drunk-driving accidents. The Insurance Institute for Highway Safety notes: "Among fatally injured passenger vehicle drivers ages 16–17, 17 percent of males and 10 percent of females in 2009 had BACs at or above 0.08 percent. Among fatally injured drivers ages 18–19, 35 percent of males and 24 percent of females had BACs at or above 0.08 percent" (IIHS 2009).

Researchers in psychology continue to try to find correlates and predictive factors for risky or self-destructive behavior (Mayton, Nagel, and Parker 1991). One study of male juniors and seniors in high school found that egocentrism, or an underestimation of the likelihood that driving while under the influence of alcohol would result in an accident or an arrest, was more common among subjects who had driven while drunk than among those who had not done so. No relationship was noted between drunk driving and knowing someone who had been involved in a traffic accident (Arnett 1990).

Many controversial issues influence drug-prevention research and the ways it is conducted, reported, and assessed. In a 1998 review of these topics, Kreft and Brown discussed selective reporting of findings, media's representation of questionable research results, masking of detrimental program effects, assuming program effectiveness rather than testing for it, and "the irrelevance of actual evidence in school-based drug prevention policy development in the past decade" (1). (These problems of methodology and representation persist today.) The authors suggested that possible solutions to the ineffectiveness of drug-prevention programming might involve emphasizing affective connectedness, rather than social skills, to reduce youth harm.

Researchers studied a program in Gloucester, Massachusetts, which built ten active coalitions around key community life systems. The ten coalitions devised activities designed to develop resiliency and reduce risk factors in young people. The results suggest that a comprehensive approach could be effective for most substance-abuse outcomes involving older high school students. But even comprehensive community-based programs have often proven unsuccessful at changing students' knowledge, attitudes, and concern about impaired driving (Shaw et al. 1997; Shope, Molnar, and Streff 1996).

A large-scale comprehensive evaluation of the California Drug Alcohol Tobacco Education (DATE) program compared forty focus-group interviews of at-risk and thriving groups in eleven high, middle, and elementary school districts, analyzing students' perception of whether drug-prevention education programs make a positive difference in their lives or are merely symbolic. From their narrative analysis, these researchers concluded that at-risk and thriving students at all three educational levels use "story" to make sense of prevention education and to distinguish use from abuse. Both at-risk and thriving high school students, this evaluation found, believed that hearing only one side of the substance-use-and-abuse story, and strict expulsion policies, further alienate those students most in need of help. These results, posited the authors of the study, could have implications for the use of narrative as an assessment tool, and for substance-use-prevention policy (D'Emidio-Caston and Brown 1998).

The most common approaches to tobacco, alcohol, and drug abuse prevention focus on providing factual information about the adverse consequences of using these substances, but the evaluation literature shows that the mix of frightening statistics and moral messages is not effective in influencing substance-use behavior (Botvin and Botvin 1997). Critics have raised objections to the manipulation and coercion of students' emotions through so-called health terrorism (Stryker 1999), contending that this type of program is more about adults wanting to control teenagers than about people working together with mutual respect and realistic goals. "I'm not aware of any good studies that show these fear-based messages work," said psychologist Timothy Marchell, director of alcohol policy initiatives at Cornell University, in a newspaper interview (Karlin 2002).

Many communities across America have implemented (and added as appendices to E15M) contracts for teens and parents to sign, such as the "Prom Promise" or SADD's "Contract for Life," or they offer a "Safe Rides" service, which gives rides home ("with no questions asked") to students who have been drinking. Safe Rides programs have sparked controversy;

although they are widely acknowledged as effective in reducing drunk driving, critics worry that they condone underage drinking. "While in concept the program goals are laudable," a MADD leader wrote in 1985, "in practice the program does not work. It is indicated that perhaps as much as 90 percent of the teenagers using such programs are in fact using it as a taxi service—not as a means of avoiding driving with a drunk driver or driving drunk themselves" (Lightner 1985). Arguing that Safe Rides programs send mixed messages to teenagers, and that MADD should not fund or monitor them, organizers called for a rethinking of this approach. They considered the parent-child contract largely ineffective, and MADD ceased to use it on a national basis. MADD's official position statement on the topic of designated drivers states, "MADD fully understands all of the harms and risks associated with underage drinking and opposes any alcohol use by those under age 21. MADD supports enforcement of underage drinking laws and therefore cannot condone safe ride programs for those under the legal drinking age" (Mothers against Drunk Driving 2011).

PREVENTION THROUGH SCARE TACTICS: SETTING THE STAGE FOR EVERY 15 MINUTES

A review of the research suggests that until communities began to stage mock accidents, no prevention programs integrated the factors of education, law enforcement, peer-led interventions, and dramatic scare tactics. Every 15 Minutes combines all of these elements; yet it has its roots in previous prevention strategies that rely on the impact of graphic imagery and sensory experience.

As drunk-driving-prevention efforts proliferated in the mid-1980s, local prevention efforts began to feature what in folklore studies might be called a "kernel" (Stahl 1989) of the eventual E15M: a wrecked car placed in front of the school at prom time as a graphic reminder of the consequences of driving drunk. This is still done in communities all over the country; sometimes the slogans and symbols of Every 15 Minutes are borrowed as well. (For example, it is not unusual for a school to set up a sign declaring the "every 15 minutes" statistic next to the crash scene.)

Even earlier scare tactics ancestors of E15M clearly appear in the Highway Safety Foundation's (HSF) productions of the 1950s and 1960s. This organization pioneered an approach to driver education in which gory color films of fatal car accidents were shown to students, combining shocking images with statistical data. The HSF's first films came out as early as 1957; most were produced between 1959 and 1977, winning many awards and becoming widely used in the American school system. (*Death on the Highway,* produced by "The Suicide Club" of Ft. Myers, Florida, also left some skid marks on the memories of young drivers.) But they were phased out during the 1980s, as schools felt the scenes of highway death were too graphic and replaced them with cartoons and crash test footage. The HSF films' reputation endured, though; *Signal 30, Wheels of Tragedy,* and others became a shared memory of those who were scarred by their nightmarish imagery. *Hell's Highway: The True Story of Highway Safety Films,* a 2003 documentary project about the films (Wood), prompted this reminiscence by the *New York Times* film critic A. O. Scott: "Highway Safety Films combined educational high-mindedness with an evident but unacknowledged ghoulishness. It was started by Richard Wayman, an Ohio accountant whose hobby was taking pictures of fatal car accidents. He soon gathered around him a group of like-minded citizens, including a police officer and a few insurance executives, who hit upon the idea of showing these shocking images to high school students to acquaint them with the horrible consequences of unsafe driving. They were, quite literally, ambulance chasers, but with a strong sense of civic mission."

In *Hell's Highway* (2003), director Bret Wood interviews film buffs who speak of the delicious anticipation of viewing the driver-ed films. These commentators allude to "a whole mythology" around the imminent traumatic screening experience: stories of teenagers who fainted or ran screaming from the room, and rumors of buckets in the aisles for vomiting. A similar rumble of eager apprehension accompanies the typical E15M event.

The documentary film's website (no longer active) invited people whose lives were touched in various ways by the HSF films to post memories. Paul Gilger's contribution highlighted an element of community interest and participation in the staging of these early "mock accidents":

> As a young child, I participated as an actor in one of the reenactments for a Highway Safety Film . . . They brought in an "official" director on that one to stage it. One of the reenactments was staged on my street . . . I was out riding my bike that day and joined the crowd watching. One of the production assistants simply came up to me and a couple of other kids and asked if we wanted to be in the film. We said, "Sure," and he said, "Okay, go stand over there in that yard with your bikes." So we did. It was very casual—no signing of any release forms. I remember the two cars screaming towards the intersection, with stunt drivers, timed to miss each other at the last second—but of

course the camera angles were set to look like they would hit. (http://cin-emaweb.com/highwaysafety)

Highway Safety Films' creation of this morbid genre perhaps foreshadowed the widespread community fascination with Every 15 Minutes' mock crashes generations later.

In the late 1970s, the documentary film *Scared Straight* brought national attention to what was promoted as a groundbreaking strategy in the effort to prevent juvenile crime through scare tactics. It was based on an experiment begun in 1976 at Rahway State Prison in New Jersey, where kids were brought in to meet inmates in the "Lifers' Group." The inmates exposed teenagers to raw and obscene language and graphic descriptions of the violence and sodomy of prison life—consequences they would face if they didn't give up their lawless ways. *Scared Straight* boasted that it had an 80 to 90 percent success rate, spurring legislators in over thirty states to replicate the "miracle" program. Part of its power apparently lay in its immediacy, as teenagers heard the sounds of cell doors slamming, smelled the odors of the prison, and were grabbed and spit upon by inmates. Many similar aspects of learning through experience appear in versions of Every 15 Minutes, where Living Dead students visit prisons, morgues, and funeral homes.

Scared Straight became a sensation after it was aired on Los Angeles television station KTLA (Channel 5) in 1978; praised by the *Los Angeles Times* as "one of the most unusual and powerful television programs ever broadcast" (Greenwood 2005, 102), it won the Academy Award that year. The evidence it presented was anecdotal and qualitative, but like many programs it inspired, it claimed to have an overwhelming impact on adolescent audiences. At the same time, it implied that the point of documented results was moot; its corporate sponsor, Signal Companies, insisted, "If televising this film helps even 10 kids go straight, then it has been worth it" (NCIA 1979). That sentiment is echoed in today's Every 15 Minutes programs, with its ubiquitous refrain: "If one life is saved, it's all worth it."

The concept of the Rahway program was not new. According to the National Center on Institutions and Alternatives (NCIA) in "Scared Straight: A Second Look" (1979), prisoners were speaking on crime and its consequences to religious, educational, and youth groups in more than twenty states as early as the 1960s, in programs such as Operation Teenager in Texas, Prison Profiles in Illinois, Don't Follow Me in Colorado, and Operation Crime Prevention in Tennessee. In notoriously intimidating presentations, prisoners told their life stories and described the realities of prison life. Evaluation of these programs, though, remained informal or incomplete. Some of them sent out surveys to former clients and reported high success rates; but so few of the participants (sometimes less than 1 percent) responded that these results were virtually meaningless. A field investigator on the Tennessee program told NCIA, "Operation Crime Prevention seemed well regarded by the persons interviewed, with responses ranging from almost unlimited enthusiasm to mild praise. No one suggested that the program is not accomplishing its goals, which include the prevention of juvenile crime. However, there has been no systematic assessment of the effects of the program, nor is any such research under way" (NCIA 1979). NCIA's survey of prevention research has concluded that such scare tactics have never been proven effective at changing either attitudes or behavior among the teenagers they target. Nonetheless, the *Scared Straight* dynasty continues to be sustained through revivals such as the 2011 spin-off, *Beyond Scared Straight,* aired by the A&E cable television network.

In a similar bloody vein, combining the firsthand shock of the prison-visiting programs with the gory horror of driver-education films, interactive Hell Houses have enjoyed booming popularity since the early 1990s (Brantley 2006; Pellegrini 2007). Now an entrenched Halloween custom in communities across the country, these walk-through ordeals engage local teenagers to enthusiastically act out graphic scenes of sin: drunk-driving accidents, gang violence, school shootings, incest, date rape, domestic abuse, suicide, abortions, and drug overdoses. A church member typically plays the role of God, sitting on a spotlighted throne and condemning unrepentant cast members to eternal damnation.

In the Hell Houses, masked and cloaked demons, gremlins, devils, archangels, and other supernatural characters abound; they act as tormenters, tour guides, and narrators for the thousands of visitors who walk through the successive rooms of the house. At the journey's end, devil and angel characters—or Jesus himself—exhort the visitors to make a choice between salvation and hell. Those who choose heaven proceed into rooms where church volunteers are waiting to pray with them.

Teenage role-players in Hell Houses dramatically demonstrate the consequences of their "bad choices." Girls scream on bloody operating tables, and demons dance around teenagers dying of AIDS, in graphic simulations that (like E15M) use creative sensory details. Fire-and-brimstone special effects heighten the sensory experience: strobe lights and smoke machines, and even crocks of burning Limburger cheese to really make it smell like hell. Common props include chicken parts used in the abortion scene, and real assault weapons employed in the school violence scenes. Promotional flyers and websites commonly bill the Hell House as the most "in-your-face, high-flyin', no denyin', death-defyin', Satan-be-cryin', keep-ya-from-fryin', no holds barred, 'cutting-edge' evangelism tool of the 90's!" In a news report, one teenager commented, "It's more scary than regular haunted houses because it's reality, not make-believe" (Lobdell 2000).

Such experiential horror houses have their roots in a 1972 project known as Scaremare, designed by the youth division of the Reverend Jerry Falwell's church in Lynchburg, Virginia. The contemporary tradition apparently originated at the Trinity Church in Cedar Hill, Texas, and Hell Houses have spread "like wildfire" in the United States, according to youth evangelical organizations such as Harvest Outreach (Lobdell 2000). The most well-known example has been staged annually in the Denver suburb of Arvada, Colorado, since 1993. In 1995 the Abundant Life Christian Center there began marketing a Hell House how-to kit, an instruction manual that includes scripts for staging various tragedies. Hundreds of churches each year use the kit, but local modifications flavor each version. For example, in communities that are dealing with rampant methamphetamine abuse, recent Hell Houses have featured harrowing depictions of this drug's destructive effects (Pellegrini 2007).

Like *Every 15 Minutes*, Hell Houses are continually evolving into unique incarnations. In the 1990s, their most harrowing and controversial scenes involved homosexuals dying of AIDS and girls having abortions; keeping up with timely political issues, some horror houses incorporated Monica Lewinsky scenes during the Clinton presidency scandal. And only months after the Columbine school shootings, teens dressed up as "Trenchcoat Warriors" were terrorizing classmates, shooting them in the head, before getting dragged off to hell by demons. Since September 11, 2001, some Hell Houses have featured scenes based on the infamous terrorist attacks. For example, a mock execution of terrorist leader Osama bin Laden was the star attraction of one Florida haunted house. According to news reports, a program organizer said, "Every year we have an execution. This year we wanted to execute someone everyone hates. A young FBI agent pummels bin Laden in his death row cell, then drags him kicking and screaming to the execution chamber before slamming him into the electric chair. The agent turns on the electricity, making sparks fly and the floor shake" (Associated Press 2001). Teenagers play the roles of the agent and bin Laden. Remarkably, in a time when experts and pundits characterized the country as traumatized, vulnerable, and fearful, people were throwing themselves with gusto into the most harrowing roles possible.

Variations on the Hell House title have included The Nightmare, Hell Stop, Final Destination, Heaven-n-Hell House, and Fire and Brimstone. A related phenomenon, Judgement House, began in 1983 in Alabama; a nine-scene pageant, it attempts to provide a Christian alternative to Halloween and bring people to Jesus. The program makes various scripts available to church groups wishing to stage their own versions. According to the Judgement House website, http://judgementhouse.org, since this evangelistic tool was created, almost 4 million people have attended presentations in thirty-four states, with about 10 percent "choosing a saving relationship with Jesus Christ for the first time." One typical pageant portrayed the real-life story of an athlete named Kelly Humphrey, who purportedly led several people to Jesus Christ before he died of melanoma. The story also included the fate of Jake, a youth who reaches Judgement House after rejecting the word of God. Although Judgement House's website officially distinguishes its events from Hell Houses by claiming to avoid graphic scenes and controversial social issues, local examples exhibit creativity that often embraces the macabre. For example, one Baptist congregation in Missouri used its Sunday school classroom to construct a horrific car accident scene whose "realism brought tears to many eyes," according to its online newsletter (http://www.fbcbutlermo.org/judgementpage_7.htm). Like Every 15 Minutes, Hell House, and other dramas, Judgement House scenarios build in current themes: recently, the tragic consequences of texting while driving have provided suitably bloody material for its narratives.

Such Christian-themed morality plays have sparked controversy and drawn wide media attention, but a 2002 documentary film by George Ratliff (2002a) was the first to present an ethnographic, in-depth look at the phenomenon through the eyes of organizers and participants. Ratliff shows how role-players compete for the most dramatic parts—for example, "Suicide Girl," who takes drugs at a rave party, gets gang-raped, and ends up committing suicide. One girl exclaims that she was nervous at first about acting out the rape scene, but that it ended up being "a lot of fun." Some of their comments underscore the entertainment appeal of prevention programs that use experiential or interactive models and techniques.

American high schools have employed other symbolic dramas to communicate and reinforce social values, transform attitudes, and control risk-taking behavior. Many such didactic rituals are informed by the fundamental educational theory that people learn best through firsthand experience. (John Dewey's 1916 essay "Democracy and Education" was a landmark contribution to the development of this "hands and minds" approach, borne out by the educational neuroscience research of the past few decades.) Among educators and activists interested in transmitting values, dramatic methods are increasingly winning support. Such efforts to make teenagers learn by experience have generated numerous examples: health class assignments in which students carry around raw eggs to gain understanding of parenthood's responsibilities have been popular for several decades, and sociologists have conducted experiments in which students wear pink triangles in order to learn tolerance (Rabow, Stein, and Conley 1999). "Simulator dolls" such as Baby Think It Over, Drug Affected Baby, and Fetal Alcohol Syndrome Manikin have aimed to prevent teenage pregnancy and parental drug abuse (Cohen 1994; Stryker 1999). The Empathy Belly, a device schools use to deter teenage pregnancy, is a thirty-pound suit with a hot-water bottle and lead weights that rest on the bladder, with sand-filled breasts completing the outfit. Girls assigned to waddle around in the Belly for a day can "experience third-trimester weight gain and back pain" as well as heartburn and constricted breathing (Marselas 2002).

Interactive methods have grown equally popular in the crusade against teenage drug and alcohol use. The National Judicial College (NJC) and the National Highway Traffic Safety Administration launched a drunk-driving-prevention campaign in 2001 with a curriculum called Courage to Live, bringing judges in to schools to hold "live" DUI hearings. The Nevada-based NJC has promoted this courtroom drama's "state of the art teaching style" (PR Newswire 2001). Striving for an attitude-adjusting "experience" of death, Reality Program, implemented in Tennessee in the 1990s, had teens watch simulated death in a hospital emergency room and then make their own funeral arrangements. As mentioned in chapter 1, role-playing student Doctors of Death have presented the consequences of drug abuse with methods comparable to E15M.

Anxieties about school shootings have generated dramatic rehearsals in high schools to prepare staff and students for potential shootings (Portner 1998). (Like drunk driving, these incidents are *perceived* to be on the rise regardless of statistics indicating the opposite; this distorted perception may result from an explosion of media coverage of the subject.) Following the events of September 11, 2001, panic about terrorist attacks spawned similar reenactments of traumatic scenarios, as schools simulated hostage crises through "lockdown drills" in which the entire school participated.

In a related theatrical genre, the one-act play *Bang Bang You're Dead* has spread throughout the country since 1999, when it was created by teacher William Mastrosimone and a group of high school students to reflect the reality of teenage alienation and gun violence. It has been adapted and produced by thousands of high schools across America as well as internationally since Mastrosimone made its script freely available online (Shea 2002).

Among these events, Every 15 Minutes has proven itself particularly fertile, mushrooming among communities of diverse sizes and character, and adapting easily to the practical, aesthetic, political, and psychic needs of each locale.

THE LIFE OF EVERY 15 MINUTES

Against this backdrop, Every 15 Minutes was a young but highly visible tradition emerging on the national scene when I began my ethnographic fieldwork. I have documented hundreds of versions of E15M in some detail, and no two reenactments of the grisly scenario are alike; yet they exhibit remarkable consistency across geographic and demographic boundaries. Their dissemination, through informal conduits and active tradition-bearers, has naturally followed unpredictable and idiosyncratic paths.

In the first stages of my research I considered applying some historic-geographic methods in the attempt to trace these paths (in the spirit of Stith Thompson's classic 1953 study [see Thompson 1965], "The Star Husband Tale," tracing a folklore form across generations). While this effort did not reveal any scientific patterns in the growth of the phenomenon, it did bring up some of the particular challenges of tracking contemporary traditions in the high school setting and in an era of mass media and Internet communication. For example, the concept of generations, in the context of school traditions, is condensed. In the case of E15M, every new class may be a generation—or, considering the interval of time between enactments of E15M and the student body's collective memory of the event, it may be more appropriate to group generations by two or four years. The size of the school and of the audience matters;

in many schools, only juniors and seniors are involved in the program, with the younger generation of underclassmen aware of the proceedings, sometimes resentful of being excluded, and anticipating their own turn to "die" when they are old enough.

With word of Every 15 Minutes spreading through multiple conduits, including both personal and mass-mediated communication, problems arise in precisely mapping the tradition's spread. The graphic drama of E15M makes it an appealing subject for television reports, and with American communities and schools increasingly Internet savvy, E15M can be quickly transmitted to a population—impossible to quantify—of spectators who experience it secondhand.

Nevertheless, E15M does have a life history, traceable in broad strokes. Growing from the program's original kernel (a wrecked car placed in front of the school), a new form began to take shape as local emergency services came to use the wrecks to simulate accident scenes, not only as scare tactic but also as a training exercise for their personnel. Not until around 1990 did the elaborated version of Every 15 Minutes appear, incorporating the two day chronology of the staged accident and its aftermath, experiential tours for the Living Dead, and mock funerals. By this time, SADD groups had proliferated: the organization boasted over 25,000 chapters throughout the United States (Coles 1998). The police department of Spokane, Washington, claims to have originated the concept of expanding the previously simple crash scenes.

According to the recollection of officials in Spokane-area police departments, by 1993, neighboring Kennewick County had picked up Every 15 Minutes. The next year it appeared for the first time in California, where Chico and other communities took the lead (and sometimes took credit for creating the program) in spreading the word.

Across the country many who are involved in local versions allude to these Washington innovators. But while some programs' written materials refer to Spokane, many people who organize E15M state that it started at the school (often a neighbor) from which they learned it. Many organizers cite California as the birthplace of E15M, often specifically naming Chico; others refer vaguely to E15M as a "national program," conferring an air of official validity upon it without specifying an origin or headquarters.

The Chico Police Department was apparently the first to secure state funding, through a grant (provided by the California Alcoholic Beverage Control Grant Assistance to Law Enforcement [GALE] program), as well as recognition for its efforts. (In 1996 the department received the Excellence in Community Policing Award from the National League of Cities.) Chico, soon followed by the cities of Cerritos and El Segundo, made documentary videos of Every 15 Minutes (copies could be ordered for about $20); ranging from thirty minutes to over an hour, the videos included footage of the program's enactment as well as interviews with organizers and role-players. These communities hired professional videographers to make their documentaries; most schools produce at least in-house montages of scenes from their events, often with student involvement in the production process. In viewing several dozen E15M videotapes made between 1999 and 2003, I noticed striking similarities as well as various creative local touches, and schools passing videos on to other schools created a significant conduit for the transmission of the tradition. Police buddies, Internet communication, local media, and countless unpredictable random encounters have carried it from one region to another, and while there are clusters and patterns, there is no scientific formula to the path of this Grim Reaper.

In the mid-1990s, examples of Every 15 Minutes began to spring up in central Pennsylvania. A new conduit developed through a website originated in Lehigh Valley, Pennsylvania, where many programs clustered. At http://every15minutes.com, which soon billed itself as the "National Headquarters," one can download a manual with tips on conducting E15M, order a two-hour documentary video, and buy products: T-shirts with an embroidered Grim Reaper logo, stickers, postcards, and lanyards (cords worn around the neck to carry keys, ID cards, etc.). Other communities have made everything from key chains to commemorative toe tags, sometimes selling them on their own websites. These artifacts both reflect and enhance the program's popularity and symbolic appeal.

(The "National Headquarters" of E15M remained somewhat mysterious to me, even after several years of researching this program's local versions around the country. If there was a staff at the headquarters, it did not respond to e-mail and only rarely to phone calls—and then only to report that the man in charge, Officer Dean Wilson, was away "on a training." I once drove to Lehigh Valley, Pennsylvania, and arrived at headquarters— with some difficulty, as only a post office box was listed on the website—to find a stark new police station building from which I was turned away with the flat response that Officer Wilson was not expected back for days and that no one else there knew any details about Every 15 Minutes. Apparently this "national organization" consists primarily of one or two representatives advising other schools on their programs, while the vast majority of E15M versions are put together in a do-it-yourself fashion, often using materials furnished by other schools or police departments but relying mostly on local interpretations, priorities, and aesthetic preferences.)

A factor in the spread of the program, and a significant window into its life history, is the http://every15minutes.com "Guestbook." This archive of viewers' comments and addresses provides a database of information—points by which one can trace the tradition's dissemination, and its continuity and change over distance and time. Guestbook contributors have provided evidence of a vast range of E15M versions and conduits across the country, belying the official tone of the "national" website. In an example of how multiple media conduits affect the transmission of the E15M idea, dozens of postings in the Guestbook referred to Casey Kasum's popular radio program, *American Top 40,* which in 1998 broadcast a listener's letter describing the simulated tragedy with a heartfelt plea against drunk driving. Morning news shows on national television also sparked comment on the Guestbook page when they produced segments about Every 15 Minutes in the late 1990s and in April 2001 (*The Today Show,* NBC-TV; Lewis 2001). Thus television, radio, and Internet media intersect and accelerate the dissemination of a tradition, in waves impossible to pinpoint or quantify exactly. In chapter 6, I will explain how the advent of YouTube and other video-sharing methods fueled this acceleration, adding a new dimension and a new conduit for this modern traditional drama.

While the range of individual experiences of the program is surely unlimited, public testimonials (on television and on the Internet) have been overwhelmingly supportive. I suspect that participants who are enthusiastic about E15M are more likely to get television reporters' attention, to write letters to the editor in local newspapers, and to post comments in a public forum such as the E15M website. In addition, the selection of Guestbook entries may also be controlled by the website's monitors, although the Lehigh, Pennsylvania, police department office sponsoring the site has no explicit policy beyond removing profanity.

Some examples of posted comments follow (I have changed the names of students cited in these quotes):

> I was one of the chaperones for the students involved in this program. What an honor it was to be asked to participate in such an outstanding program. We all know kids drink. We are not that naive. To be able to be part of a program that has an effect on so many lives was an awesome responsibility.

This is a program that will not be soon forgotten. If we can reach one teen-ager and save the everlasting grief of parents we have done our best as adults. (California, February 12, 2002)

I took part in this program last year. Seeing how this affects others around you gives you a feeling of how people react to such trauma. Being a part of it has made me see how dangerous and stupid drinking and driving is. Seeing pictures of accidents and seeing people in the morgue has made me promise myself to never drink and drive. (Texas, January 29, 2002)

I don't think that there could be anything more real and traumatic than this program. I had some friends involved in the program, and I thought it was kind of silly. I didn't really know what to expect going to school that day. Right off, in first period, one of my best friends was declared dead and taken out of the class. Before I knew it, tears were rolling down my face, and I started to realize what this program was all about. I didn't understand— I knew it was fake and that she really wasn't dead, but for some reason, I couldn't hold back my mournful emotions. For the rest of the day until lunch, my friends and I would be walking down the hall and see another "dead" classmate, and break down into tears. My friends and I actually got really close up to the accident. We saw Greg get out of his truck and stumble around as he got arrested and taken away by the police. We then noticed something moving in the mangled car next to us. It was Karen, our class president and good friend. She started screaming bloody murder, and bawl-ing . . . They weren't moving, and there faces were covered in blood. My friends and I were all sobbing at this point. As the medi-copter and coroner arrived, things set in even more. The community had gone really far to make this real for us! As we saw Rob's mom collapse in the police officer's arms, we all sobbed even more. The next day was the funeral. As the bagpipes played and the pallbearers brought in the two coffins, we all started crying yet again. There was a slide show presented to us, and at the end, Rob and Karen's voices appeared from the sound system. They were reading the letters they had written to their family and friends. When we finally got to see them again, it was like I hadn't seen them in years! This program is unbelievably effective. I give two thumbs up to the creators, and a big bravo goes to the community for bringing it to us. (Maine, January 30, 2002)

By 2003, any Internet search resulted in plenty of examples of Every 15 Minutes sites mounted by schools or police or fire departments. A large per-centage of the E15M websites currently viewable belong to California high schools. Many previously existing sites have become inactive, but this is no reliable indicator of the program's vitality and popularity, as sites depend on maintenance and funding by the sponsoring schools or police departments.

A typical E15M site features a description of the event's format, photos, and graphic design portraying the Grim Reaper. websites also may include video clips, inspirational poems, message boards for posting comments, obituaries of the Living Dead, advice for replicating the program, and purported drunk-driving statistics. The fifteen minutes number is prominent, in varying renditions. The following statements, for example, appeared on Internet sites accessed during the autumn of 2003:

- "Every 15 Minutes someone in the United States dies in an alcohol related crash." (http://www.niagarapal.com/every-15Minutes.htm)
- "According to statistics, every 15 minutes in the United States someone is either killed or seriously injured in a drunk driving accident." (http://losangeles.cbslocal.com/)
- "According to a National Highway Traffic Safety Administration statistic, someone in the United States dies or is injured in an alcohol or drug-related collision every 15 minutes." (http://www.mcso.us/public/)
- "Every 15 minutes, someone, somewhere, dies from an alcohol-related vehicle crash." (http://www.hesperiastar.com)
- "The program's name is a result of the fact that a teenager is injured or killed in an alcohol-related accident in the United States every 15 minutes." (http://www.currentargus.com)
- "Student volunteers throughout the day were pulled out of their classes to dress in black shirts, paint their faces and then return to class unable to speak to represent the average of one person killed in Texas every 15 minutes by a drunk driver." (http://www.zwire.com)

While some colleges have adopted Every 15 Minutes, it remains primarily a prevention tactic targeted at high school populations. This may be due to the perceived importance of "seeing your friends die," as college student bodies are typically larger and less tightly connected than the enforced communities of high schools. A notable exception, the Naval Safety Center in California, has a restricted military environment. This academy's 2001 website introduced "a new program unveiled late last year by Naval Station, San Diego. The program is designed to reduce the number of Sailors and Marines we're losing in alcohol-related car crashes. Even after all the lectures and training these men and women have attended, they still succumb to the dangers of drinking and driving" (http://safetycenter.navy.mil/). The

Naval Station's adaptation of the program used military imagery and theatrics, as depicted in website photos showing a bagpipe player, honor guard, gun salute, and rows of white government-issue tombstones.

My research of newspaper archives throughout the United States indicates that, by the late 1990s, examples of Every 15 Minutes appeared in at least twenty-five states, and they were multiplying quickly in California, Oregon, Washington, Pennsylvania, Maryland, New Mexico, and Texas. By 2003, I had identified examples in nearly every state, with California, Pennsylvania, and Maryland the most fertile ground in the cultivation and propagation of the program. In the early stages of my research, I created a data sheet with all the traits, or points of variation, I had come across until then; I used this template as a starting point for interviews (on site and by telephone) with organizers of Every 15 Minutes across the country.

KEY ELEMENTS AND VARIATIONS WITHIN EVERY 15 MINUTES

Having gathered several dozen examples in this manner, I began to conceptualize something close to a "complete version" of E15M, comprising key structural and aesthetic elements. Still, new motifs and variations continually presented themselves, and many of these will be discussed in later chapters. As with any form of folklore, E15M evolves as it is passed on through personal, social, and media conduits. Localized versions exhibit both stability and variation, neither of which can be separated from the human and contextual factors that surround the program's enactments. "We copied it from this other school, but we changed it—we have our own version here," said one informant who organized the event in her Maryland community; hers was a typical comment. Participants I have interviewed express conviction as to the "right" way to do things (based on what they learned from E15M publicity or from another tradition-bearer), yet they also speak with pride about the uniqueness and originality of their own school's event. "Our school and [a neighboring school] are the only schools, around here and maybe even in the whole country, to do a program like this. We should spread it to other schools!" asserted a boy to his fellow Living Dead members at their Maryland retreat.

These tradition-bearers consistently cite elements and details whose presence and sequence they consider essential for the effectiveness of the program. What aspects of Every 15 Minutes are crucial to the event?

Below, I have broken down E15M into key structural elements, each subject to infinite variation.

The Grim Reaper

Every program features a Grim Reaper character who pulls students from their classrooms to represent victims of drunk driving.

Variations include: the criteria by which "reaped" students are selected; whether parents must be involved for students to participate; the total number of students selected for reaping; whether they are referred to as "Living Dead" or "Walking Dead"; what sound over the public address system indicates a death: gong/bell tolling/heartbeat to flatline; who plays the Grim Reaper; whether he carries a scythe or a staff; if the Grim Reaper speaks to students or is silent; if Death's face is veiled or visible; whether there can be more than one Grim Reaper; whether students know in advance they are to be reaped, or what class they will be pulled from.

The Living Dead

Every program designates a group of students to portray the dead and go on a retreat, separated from their friends and family.

Variations include: color and style of T-shirts; what makeup is used, for example, white face paint, eyes blacked out, tears painted on cheeks; the accessories included, such as coroner's tags, crosses, signs worn around necks, halos; whether the Living Dead are allowed to return to class or are removed permanently; whether they are allowed to speak to no one, or only to teachers; whether their parents must be involved, or give permission for participation.

Obituaries, Cemetery

Every program includes obituaries for the "dead" and often other forms of public memorialization.

Variations include: who writes the obituaries, parents, students, or police; whether photos accompany obituaries; if they are read aloud in classrooms by a police officer or delivered over the PA system; where they are posted—in classrooms, the school foyer, the school website/newspaper/cable television; how long obituaries remain posted; whether the graveyard is constructed on school grounds, and if it is constructed gradually throughout day or all at once.

Death Notifications to Parents

In every program, parents of the Living Dead receive notifications of their children's "deaths."

Variations include: who notifies the parents of the death; how many police go to the house; whether a chaplain accompanies the police; whether notifications are filmed; whether the police go to workplaces as well as homes.

Mock Accident

Every program features a mock accident scene at which the student body is the audience and students play the roles of victims and drunk drivers.

Variations include: whether a 911 call is broadcast over the PA system; the location of the crash—school parking lot, football field, track, driveway; which classes attend as audience; whether spectators are standing or in bleachers; if tarps cover the cars before the scene begins; the number of cars and students in the crash; the gender of the drunk driver; whether victims are screaming or silent; if parents and townspeople attend; if the audience is aware in advance or surprised; whether parental permission slips are required for students to attend the crash scene; the extent of emergency services responding to scene, such as the Jaws of Life being employed or a helicopter evacuation; whether a narrator is present to explain events as emergency personnel work; whether sobriety tests are given to the drunk driver, and if he or she resists or complies, is handcuffed or not; if beer bottles are visible on the scene; if students are dressed up as if for prom.

Victim's Death at the Hospital

Every program includes the death of a student role-player from the mock accident.

Variations include: whether one or two parents go to the hospital; if the student dies in front of his or her parents; if the scene is filmed for video; if the doctor tells parents about procedures used to try to save child; whether parents must identify the body; if the student's hand is placed in ice to make it cold to touch; if parents are asked to make decision about organ donation.

Tours for the Living Dead

Every program takes the group of Living Dead students away from their school to visit sites related to the consequences of drunk driving.

Variations include: whether tours are conducted in one group or two; if "crash victims" accompany the group or go separately to the hospital;

how many tours the Living Dead experience, including tours of prisons, police stations, courthouses, emergency rooms morgues, funeral homes; whether adults (counselors/parents/organizers/police) accompany the group as chaperones.

Retreat for the Living Dead, Letters to Parents

Every program takes the group of Living Dead away overnight to an isolated location, where students do activities including writing letters from beyond the grave.

Variations include: the location of the retreat, whether a hotel or another venue; what games are played; if and what bonding exercises are enacted; whether real victims or emergency personnel participate as guest speakers; who acts as chaperone; whether the format of the letters to parents is prescribed or open; whether letters can be written to people other than parents; whether students read their letters aloud at the retreat; whether their parents meanwhile write letters too, jointly or separately; whether students make a voluntary decision to read their letters at the assembly; whether all who want to read their letters are allowed to, or whether they are selected by organizers; how much leisure time the Living Dead get before bedtime; whether chaperones sleep in rooms with the students.

Assembly/Mock Funeral

Every program continues on the second day with an assembly at school and the return of the Living Dead.

Variations include: where the assembly takes place, in the gymnasium or auditorium; whether the Living Dead are still in face paint; whether and when students and parents exchange letters; the number of letters read aloud; what other presentations are made by guest speakers and officials; whether the Living Dead and/or their parents give testimonials; whether the assembly has coffins, candles, flowers, and if the Living Dead are lying under sheets or lined up onstage; whether there is music: bugles playing taps, the choir singing, or other music; if students file past an open coffin with a mirror inside; if there is a school viewing of the program's videotape; if the assembly ends with students signing a pledge/contract not to drink and drive; whether the Living Dead are formally reunited with parents at a post-assembly reception, with food; whether the Living Dead are allowed to go home after assembly or must attend the rest of the school day.

Evaluation

Every program includes some form of evaluation, formal or informal.

Variations include: the existence of a post-program meeting; whether all students or only Living Dead students complete a survey; whether class discussions of the event are conducted; if there is media attention and comment; whether arrangements are made for postings on an Internet message board.

As Every 15 Minutes migrates and becomes a tradition in more and more communities, it changes to reflect its context in a number of ways. In places where most of the parents work, fewer mock death notifications are given, as people are often reluctant to have their workplaces interrupted by this drama. In one small rural town, eight students were packed into the wrecked cars "to make it more real," because in that area few kids had cars and most drove around in large groups. The fire department coordinator of a tiny Texas town told me that their school didn't have enough kids to "reap" one every fifteen minutes all day long, so they selected members of the community to be part of the Living Dead—making the impact all the more real, he said. "We killed off the owner of the Pizza Hut!"

In some schools, an *actual* drunk-driving crash or other tragedy sometimes causes the program to be modified or completely abandoned after months of planning. One week after the shootings at Columbine, an Illinois town did decide to hold its long-planned Every 15 Minutes but toned down much of the imagery in order to make it "more symbolic and less traumatic," its organizer told me. For example, the Grim Reaper was canceled but a policeman pulled kids from classes, the Living Dead wore T-shirts but no face paint, and the obituaries the parents had written were not posted. In one California community, after four drunk-driving deaths within two months, organizers debated whether to follow through with E15M. "We didn't want to re-traumatize people," a minister told the local newspaper, but in the end counselors and students decided to go ahead with the plans. "The feeling was they didn't want to let [the victims'] death go for nothing, that they had died purposelessly—but rather seize this opportunity. Even in death, to give their death some meaning and dignity" (Juneau 2000). One Internet message board posting (by a California student who had portrayed the drunk driver in the mock crash) recounted: "One week prior to the simulation there was an actual drunk-driving accident involving two of our high school students and two of our former students. I think that because of the actual accident that happened, it made the simulation more life like" (www.every15minutes.com/questbook).

The overnight retreat is conducted in a variety of ways, ranging from an intense emotional ordeal to a more casual fun-and-games approach. Sometimes it is held at the school rather than at a hotel; sometimes instead of going on a retreat, members of the Living Dead simply spend the night at a friend's house to simulate the separation from their families. The schoolwide assembly on Day Two varies according to the particular aspects of that school's version.

The program also varies and evolves based on aesthetic tastes. The T-shirts worn by the Living Dead are usually black with white lettering and designs (skeletons, heartbeat monitor lines, broken windshields, clocks with hands marking fifteen minutes). An administrator in New Mexico told me her school had used gray T-shirts last year and that it hadn't worked at all. "It was too passive," she said. "It didn't make them a part of this whole *drama*." This year, she explained, they would use black, which makes the Dead look "much more real."

Some groups of Living Dead are adorned with halos or wear miniature tombstones around their necks; their white face paint may be embellished with black tears, scars, or hollowed-out eyes. The music accompanying the mock funeral is often a popular tearjerker such as Sarah McLachlan's "I Will Remember You," or it may be the school choir singing "Amazing Grace" or a bugler playing taps. Coffins and flowers are everywhere at some schools, while others consider this tacky. But the slightest change in circumstances can alter the plans. The police coordinator in Bryan, Texas, told me, "We wanted to do coffins, but at the last minute the funeral home reneged so we didn't get the coffin, but we're going to work with a different funeral home this year." The coffin may be draped in the school colors and guarded by the local ROTC (Reserve Officers' Training Corps) club.

The SADD website urges high school clubs to organize their own "Grim Reaper Day," using the thirty-three minutes statistic, and allowing them to leave out the entire aspect of the expensive mock accident. On a now-inactive Web link, SADD offered these suggestions:

For a new twist on "Grim Reaper Day" try an "Angel of Death Day."

Gabriel, dressed in his white robe and gray beard, enters the classroom blowing his trumpet while an angel dressed in a flowing robe and gold halo

prepares students. The angel places a halo on victims' heads and also places
an angel around their neck and sprinkles them with angel dust (gold glit-
ter) . . . You might want to consider turning a hall or foyer in your school
into a morgue. As students leave the building they view the bodies covered
with the sheets and bearing toe tags. This is one way of bringing a strong
conclusion to this vivid dramatization. (www.saddonline.com/campaigns2.
htm#grim, accessed October 2003)

I considered many perspectives and elements in trying to determine
which examples qualified as Every 15 Minutes, and which were merely trun-
cated versions, lacking the elaborate role-play and the structured, progressive journey of the Living Dead. (An observer might choose to interpret
these journeys as ritual-like, as they incorporate separation, public grieving,
and cathartic reunion with the community the next day.) Some schools continued to simply place a wrecked car in front of the school, yet adopted the
Every 15 Minutes slogan; other schools produced the entire two-day event
but called it by another name. In fact, quite a few variants developed during
the same time period that E15M was beginning to proliferate: Operation
Cool, Ghost Day, Ghost Out, Black Day, Operation Prom Night, Project
Graduation, White Out, Hope Lost, and The Journey Beyond are all cousins to E15M. Often, these variants have omitted key motifs of Every 15
Minutes, such as the students' letters to parents. But in Texas, the Shattered
Dreams program replicates faithfully the basic form of Every 15 Minutes.
The man who directed Shattered Dreams in Burleson, Texas, told me
that they changed the title from Every 15 Minutes because "now it's every
twenty-two minutes." When I mentioned that the accurate statistic (at that
time) was thirty-two minutes, he replied, "Whatever."

The Every 15 Minutes title is clearly one key element of this program,
even though its accuracy is many years out of date. The fact that most
schools prefer to keep the same title, and the constant emphasis on the
"every 15 minutes" number, reveals its power and stability as a symbol. I
have asked administrators why they don't change it to reflect the latest figures. "It just wouldn't hit home as hard," they say. One Maryland teacher
explained that if the number ever got up to, say, every forty-five minutes,
then he would certainly agree to change it, but not till then. A police coordinator in Los Angeles joked that he would change it if it got to forty-seven
minutes, then turned serious: "I don't know, that's a good question. Maybe
every sixty minutes . . . [but] when you pull a student out every fifteen minutes, it's *so* dramatic. Every hour would be—I think—it would lose impact."

Exceptions do exist: one New Jersey school called its program Every 30 Minutes in June 2000. But in general, the dominance of the title figure "15" remains uncontested. In addition, the growing name recognition of Every 15 Minutes has contributed to the slogan's endurance and appeal.

Misleading statistics may persist, in fact thrive, on the well-intentioned zeal of advocates, Joel Best, author of the 2001 book *Damned Lies and Statistics: Untangling Numbers from the Media, Politicians and Activists*, remarked in an interview with the *New York Times* (Cohen 2001). Asked whether figures are misrepresented on purpose, Best explained: "Really cynical manipulation is not as important as enthusiasm, people believing that their particular concern is a legitimate one and here are some numbers that support that." He added, "Bad statistics are harder to kill than vampires."

PERCEPTIONS OF SUCCESS

Evaluating the effect of any prevention program is inherently problematic. Many schools have handed out surveys to students after Every 15 Minutes, or tracked local traffic safety statistics. Leaky, idiosyncratic methodology and vague questions, however, have produced questionable results and easily manipulated figures. A 1997 study found that substance-use-prevention programs appear to have a "paradoxical" effect; the study's quantitative results showed drug use increasing after the implementation of a drug education program, but the authors did not attempt to explain why (Furlong et al. 1997).

In the only study that any researcher had published regarding Every 15 Minutes as of 2010, Judy Bordin of the Child Development Program at California State University at Chico undertook a survey that aimed to determine the effectiveness of the program (2003). This "quantitative" study, released in February 2001, was cited with reverence by a regional coordinator of Every 15 Minutes programs in California, in conversation with me and in answer to any questions or doubts voiced by administrators or potential organizers. He recommended the study as empirical proof of E15M's value, and the Every15Minutes.com website has posted the results prominently, as did the California Department of Alcoholic Beverage Control while it was bankrolling E15M in schools throughout the state. The methodology and results of this survey are curious. During the 1999–2000 school year 1,198 students who participated in E15M as the Living Dead or who played roles in the crash scene filled out questionnaires before and after the program (with wide-ranging delays between the pre- and post-tests). They were asked to rate their likeliness to engage in drinking and driving behaviors. With every behavior listed, the students reported what Bordin and her coauthors call "statistically significant" positive change. According to the results posted on the E15M website, the following improvements occurred:

- Students decreased their number of daily and weekly drinking episodes
- Students were less likely to drive when they had drunk three or more drinks
- Students were less likely to be a passenger with a driver who had been drinking
- Students were more likely to worry about how much their friends were drinking
- Students were more likely to prevent their drinking friends from driving
- Students were more likely to talk with their parents and/or a teacher about drinking
- Students were more likely to designate a nondrinking driver
- Students were more likely to buckle their seat belts
- Students were more likely to monitor their own intake of alcohol
- Students were more likely to call for a ride home rather than drink and drive
- Students were more likely to choose not to drink
- Students were more likely to take someone's keys or hand over their keys if drinking
- Students were less likely to engage in drinking games
- Students were less likely to binge drink
- Students were more likely to walk home rather than drive
- Students were more likely to get a ride home rather than drink and drive
- Students were more likely to write a contract with their parents regarding circumstances of drinking and driving behavior

In addition, the survey asked students to "rate the meaningfulness" of different parts of Every 15 Minutes. In order of "most meaningful" to "least meaningful," on a scale from one to five, respondents rated these elements as follows:

- Assembly: 4.02
- Learning about the grief process: 3.68
- Retreat: 3.53
- Understanding my own vulnerability: 3.46
- Legal aspects of drinking and driving: 3.42
- Hearing from professionals: 3.41
- Collision scene/arrest: 3.33
- Obituary: 3.00
- Being pulled out of class: 2.44

The study also derives "statistically significant results" from participating parents: they reported themselves "more prepared to control or
prevent alcohol problems" and "more confident [their] teenager does not
drink and drive." The skewed sample used by this survey (all respondents
were active in E15M, many selecting themselves for the program), the
unreliability of self-reported behavior, the inconsistent methods of dis-
tributing and collecting the surveys, and the reliance on vague, undefined
concepts such as "meaningful" render these results extremely questionable.

Jeff Stryker, in a 1999 *New York Times* essay, makes a point not
addressed by most drunk-driving-prevention programs: "Some teenagers
may see a certain cachet in danger and risk." This factor may be consid-
erable in programs like Every 15 Minutes, but I have found virtually no
public discussion of the implications of the intensive attention paid to the
Living Dead. Teenagers prone to self-destructive behavior may have issues
of low self-esteem and feeling alienated and unappreciated, experts argue
(Ponton 1997). Could the prospect of having their eulogies read at a tearful school assembly and their tombstones wept over by classmates motivate these students in directions different from the direction that educators intend? The statistical "effectiveness" of E15M is beyond the scope
of this book. But my account reveals important aspects of the experience
participants are really having, and its often dark or unsanctioned appeal.
At every E15M event I have attended, I heard comments such as "Hey,
I wanna be dead! Grim Reaper, pick *me!*" grumbled, giggled, or yelled
through the hallways as the sinister figure made his rounds.

Despite the lack of provable results, all the E15M programs I encountered laid claim to its positive effects. This program has widespread appeal
for many reasons, including the fact that liberals and conservatives alike
can agree on desired outcomes and relate to the concern it addresses.

People want to support or fund the effort—doing so makes their businesses look good and shows they care about their community. The inherent drama of the staged accident creates a ready-made media event, providing great publicity for the program and its targeted problem. Whatever its measurable statistical outcome, interviewees tell me that the process of implementing Every 15 Minutes involves them in a community-building process. Teenagers, parents, educators, police officers, and health care workers, who might have seen one another as adversaries, say that the preparation and performance of this drama forges bonds of respect, emotion, and empathy.

All these reasons, however, do not fully explain the hold with which this phenomenon has gripped participants across the nation. The issue of drunk driving has cast an enormous emotional shadow on the American landscape, and the shadow is readily distorted. Through the flood of ambiguous and contradictory statistical data, we see people exaggerate numbers and mix quantitative evidence with rhetoric. Often with apparent belief and passion, they defend and justify prevention programs in which they have emotional, political, or financial investments.

As a folklorist observing examples of E15M as emerging events, I can search for clues as to how the program works in terms of its appeal, but I cannot provide an answer to "how well it works" in terms of cause-and-effect DUI prevention. Researchers in educational settings can easily be tempted to let their own cause-and-effect expectations about phenomena get in the way of accessing and documenting students' own point of view (Ashworth and Lucas 2000). I have not followed participants home to their family lives, attended their keg parties, sat in the passenger seat as they made life-changing decisions, or probed their psychological states and issues. (Compelling questions await researchers from fields such as psychology, adolescent development, and social policy who might delve into this topic.) But I have listened to their voices, amplified by the public address system and transmitted from one school to the next. My observations, over the following chapters, will incorporate expressions spoken into the microphone as well as some whose muttered dissent does not fit into the official story. Based on this evidence and the undeniable spread of E15M (part of a national trend toward disturbing reenactments as educational and prevention tactic), this book addresses the broad yet peculiar appeal of playing at tragedy and practicing public grief. There is no answer to whether E15M is a "good" or a "bad" idea, but my study provides striking insight into a striking phenomenon: in high schools across America, people are celebrating the lives of "dead" friends, sons, and daughters; and the hypothetically deceased are tearfully attending their own funerals.

3

Marked for Death
Ambiguity and Slippery Steps in Frames of Play

Ah, if he could only die temporarily! But the elastic heart of youth cannot be compressed into one constrained shape long at a time. Tom presently began to drift insensibly back into the concerns of this life again . . . The idea of being a clown recurred to him now, only to fill him with disgust. For frivolity and jokes and spotted tights were an offense, when they intruded themselves upon a spirit that was exalted into the vague august realm of the romantic.

—Mark Twain, *The Adventures of Tom Sawyer*

FRAMING THE REALM OF PLAY

IN SCHOLARLY STUDIES OF PLAY, "FRAMING" HAS BEEN used to understand how individuals make sense of their activities and interactions and how, based on their interpretations of frame, people communicate and express themselves in ways that can lead to collective action. In his 1955 essay "A Theory of Play and Fantasy," Gregory Bateson explained the idea of play frame in terms of the relationship of a message to its referent, as a map relates to its territory. Players communicate signals meaning, "This is play," forming the message, "These actions in which we now engage do not denote what those actions for which they stand would denote" (41). As Bateson put it, "The picture frame tells the viewer that he is not to use the same sort of thinking in interpreting the picture that he might use in interpreting the wallpaper outside the frame" (47). "Metacommunication" is Bateson's term for the frame markers that identify a space as part of the game or play, labeling it as play.

Erving Goffman, whose 1974 *Frame Analysis* was another foundational work in play theory, stated that any given situation can be seen as a "strip of

DOI:10.7330/9780874218923.c03

activity" (10) bounded by frames that actors shift and manipulate through "keying" practices. The key, Goffman's central concept in frame analysis, is a "process of transcription" of the "set of conventions by which a given activity, one already meaningful in terms of some primary framework, is transformed into something patterned on this activity but seen by the participants to be something quite else" (43–44). Keying allows people to signal, through words and behavior, what frame of action is being invoked at a given moment. Furthermore, writes Goffman, a frame can have multiple rekeyings, with "no obvious limit to the number of rekeyings to which a particular strip of activity can be subject," and each rekeying adds a "layer or lamination" to the activity (80–81).

Goffman has also developed the idea of "footing" (in the context of verbal interaction) as a means of framing; through changes in footing, he proposed, people reach a shared understanding of "what is going on here."

Usually people do not simply change footing, but instead embed one footing within another. Experiences are characterized by increases and decreases
in layering, as well as "movement closer to or further from the 'literal'"
(Goffman 1981, 154).

Scholars have seen play as an abstract realm, distinct from not-play,
with different organization, logic, and rules. The very attempt to define
frames of play implies that these realms are both exclusive and inclusive; that
is, that we can always locate ourselves and others in a clearly defined frame.
But many scholars have recognized that frames are fluid, overlapping and
mixing, and that relationships within them show continuities with people's
everyday roles in the realm outside the frame. For example, anthropologist Marjorie Goodwin has described continuities between girls' interaction occurring during jump rope play and their interaction outside the play
frame (1985). A complex communicative event such as Every 15 Minutes
involves elaborate combinations and shifts of frame, multiple experiences
with endless layers, and plenty of paradoxes. Frame analysis is a useful tool
for examining this phenomenon, just as it has contributed to studies of
games, festival, discourse, and performance.

Richard Bauman, writing of artistic performances, states, "Performance
usually suggests an aesthetically marked and heightened mode of communication, framed in a special way and put on display for an audience" (1992,
41). As Brian Sutton-Smith has pointed out, understanding this framing is
useful for the study of any kind of play, as "most social play has an audience
at least of the other players, who are monitoring the play" (1997, 192).
Sutton-Smith praises those who have extended the concept of performance
to cover ordinary play, including "any public cultural events in which community members come together to participate . . . [T]hese events of play,
games, and festivals will be more highly focused and framed, yet more
redundant and stylized than other areas of experience" (193).

MARKERS

Scholars use various terms to describe the markers that identify frames
of play: cues, signs, limits, boundaries, or brackets in time and space. These
are signals we look for and recognize, not only in formal analysis of phenomena but also in everyday life. All over the world, people use clues to
"distinguish the really real from make-believe, the indicative from the subjunctive," writes Margaret Drewal (1992) in her study of play and agency

among Yoruba tribes in Nigeria. She refers to "a drive to isolate and identify the boundaries of situations so as to contain and control them, thereby preventing slippages and keeping the really real distinguishable from play, the serious from the unserious" (16). Donald Cosentino (1982), observing Mende storytelling events in West Africa, has identified verbal conventions, narrative formulae, and theatrical devices (such as music, lighting, and costuming) that provide borders for performances. Still, Cosentino notes that accidents beyond the intention of the storyteller, and responses emerging from the audience, render these events fluid and dialectical, an ever-evolving kaleidoscope of dramatic story.

What are the signals that frame experience and activity during Every 15 Minutes events? They include markers of time, space, sound, costume, speech, touch, and other modes of expression. The markers have varying degrees of prominence within the larger context of the school environment.

As a whole event, E15M is limited by temporal and spatial markers: its two-day duration and its physical setting in the school and community define its boundaries. Within the activity of the program, internal brackets of time mark out discrete segments most obviously, the fifteen-minute intervals at which the Grim Reaper chooses his victims, but also including class periods, guided tours, time allotted for retreat activities and letter writing, and curfews and wake-up calls at the hotel.

Rules or expectations of conduct for participants serve as markers within the program (embedded within the already-existing rules of behavior in the school and community, as well as the expectations of behavior that community members already hold, based on their relationships with the participants in their real lives). But the rules can be open ended at times, depending often on the flexibility of the organizers and administrators who set them. According to the generally prescribed plan, students are not allowed to speak when they return to class as the Living Dead. This rule is not necessarily inflexible, though. It may be suspended at will by teachers needing to communicate with students about homework or tests, by other school personnel including coaches and counselors, and by the Living Dead themselves, whose cooperation or resolve may lapse under the strain of the imposed silence.

For their mock accident scenes, many large schools restrict the spectacle to an audience of selected classes (seniors only, or seniors and juniors). Such limits on who may participate as spectators, however, are also open ended in practice. In my observations, students excluded from the chosen audience leaned out the windows of their classrooms, stopped to watch as they arrived late to school, and skipped class entirely to attend the event (sometimes with the permission or encouragement of teachers who considered E15M more important than the day's academic lesson). While such actions and actors remain within the general frame of E15M (simply being present and aware of the proceedings places them within the frame), they bend and improvise on particular rules. This also indicates a general sense of holiday, or time out of time, when rules are not binding but freely ignored or transgressed.

Similar shifting of parameters may occur at the retreat for the Living Dead. The teenagers supposedly are prohibited from making phone calls to their friends and family, but this boundary is permeable in the case of urgent need. Valid exceptions are defined as such by the participants in the moment; justifications for phone calls range from requests that a student's forgotten contact lens solution be brought to the hotel to reminders to parents about the next morning's assembly. During the retreat, the Living Dead are typically required to participate in the activities, which consist primarily of bonding and visualization exercises, discussions with guest speakers about their actual drunk-driving tragedies, and the task of writing letters to their families from "beyond the grave." But I have seen this rule put aside without hesitation as individual students rush from the room in tears. (Usually a counselor will pursue them with Kleenex, but the distraught students may or may not be pressured to return to the room immediately.) In these and other areas, the limits of time and space imposed on elements within the prescribed scenario are moved and crossed for circumstantial reasons, and such tinkering happens both with and without permission from the official rule makers.

In addition to the adjustability of internal frame markers, we can notice the open-ended nature of the larger frame of time and space that defines an E15M event. For example, E15M in its entirety may include postmortem evaluations and comments, especially if something unexpectedly noteworthy or controversial happened. "It's still the talk of the town," one organizer e-mailed me two weeks after her school's program, during which an argument had arisen between the Living Dead and the principal, who had cut their speeches short so the assembly would not run later than scheduled. Internet message boards—the Every15Minutes.com Guestbook in the early days and, more recently, Facebook groups or YouTube videos created in conjunction with various E15M events—buzz for days or weeks about the power of the program. Guestbook postings, dominated by the typical comments about how "emotional," "impactful," and "real" the program was, may be constrained too—frame limits are imposed by webmasters who monitor and edit comments to suit the organizers' conception of appropriate feedback. Those standards are not always explicitly stated, but they influence the content of the Guestbook and could discourage expressions of dissent. (In chapter 6, I will discuss the more free-ranging and contested discourse that has emerged on websites independent of Every15Minutes.com's auspices, yet often including commentary from local organizers and producers.)

Some markers are directly observable, striking the senses with resounding signals that "this is play." Identity markers as mundane as T-shirts carry meaning, and the elements of costume that adorn E15M participants include the black shirts of the Living Dead, their armbands and lanyards and toe tags, and the cloak and scythe of the Grim Reaper. Costuming also includes the standard apparel of the emergency personnel playing their own roles in the reality-based fiction. The face makeup of the Living Dead, of course, is a telling marker of identity and play frame. The process of face painting occurs in a special area set aside for this purpose, where designated makeup artists or volunteers facilitate the symbolic transition of the "reaped" teenagers from their previous lives as students to their temporary new identity as the dearly departed. The entire scene in the makeup room, encompassing costume, location, timing, activity, and specialized roles, marks a departure from the everyday context.

Likewise, the students chosen to be "crash victims" undergo a transition as their elaborate wounds are designed by moulage artists. Once rendered suitably maimed and bloody, the role-players serve to mark the fact that the play scenario is under way. But the embedded nature of this play frame is crucial; the participants observing the realistic wreckage and injuries know to interpret it as play, thanks to a number of wider frame markers. Such markers may include, for example, the disaster's location on the football field; prom clothes worn by the car occupants; the implausible broadcasting of sound effects (screeching brakes, then shattering glass and metal) over the intercom; and most important, the references by all involved to the impending event for days or weeks in advance. Thus, participants in general understand how to interpret the image of their bleeding peers slumped in totaled cars: simultaneously as action removed from the realm of the everyday, and as nonliteral action still embedded in the everyday context of school parking lots, football fields, lunch periods, and public address systems.

This illustrates the point that frames of play are defined both from the inside and from the outside (Lindquist 2001). A scene at which firefighters pry a car apart with the Jaws of Life would not be recognizable as play apart from the incongruous surroundings, the spectators and their buzz of informal discourse, and markers like announcements and voice-overs, T-shirts and tables stocked with snacks and soda. Many of the markers that bracket this play about death are understood not to be taken literally because they stand out in disorienting contrast with elements in the larger frame. For instance, at an East Los Angeles high school, twenty gravestones for the Living Dead were set up in the courtyard among the fast-food kiosks that serve lunch. Students lining up for Taco Bell burritos did not appear at all fazed by the somber display. On an in-school cable television station in Maryland, student anchors read death announcements, then immediately segued into the update on the varsity baseball team. Striding down the hallways of a suburban Southern California school, the Grim Reaper and four obituary-laden cops were accompanied by a jovial entourage of about fifteen counselors, parent volunteers, police, and community-service coordinators—all munching on donuts and craning their necks for a glimpse of students' reactions to the reaping. And after one school's mock crash, during the last class period of the day, an update on the injured victims' condition was read over the public address system along with the charges being filed against the drunk driver: "two counts of homicide by motor vehicle while intoxicated, and one count of causing a life-threatening injury. If convicted, he could face up to thirty-seven years in the penitentiary. Thank you."

Intercom systems in schools, and loudspeakers at crash scenes and assemblies, amplify a variety of sounds serving as markers within E15M; these may stand out as unusual in the high school setting. Sound effects evoking a car crash often are chosen to signal the beginning of the mock accident scene. While relatively few schools incorporate that particular effect, most do play an eerie soundtrack over the public address system at fifteen-minute intervals to accompany the arrival of the Grim Reaper in the next classroom. Schools use common themes for these soundtracks— a thumping heartbeat followed by the monotone whine of a heart monitor, or a gong being struck, or musical strains from a horror movie, or a deep voice chanting "Every fifteen minutes"—but each school may create its own recording. During the mock crash scene, the emergency workers who extricate and tend to the victims, and the police who interrogate the drunk driver, may wear microphones so that every aspect of their effort is audible to the audience. As they regard the mock crash partly as a training exercise, the paramedics and firefighters tend not to add extra drama to their activities; their interactions are among the most literally realistic of the program. Yet the amplification of their grunts and comments adds another marker that this is play, not real trauma. (The strangeness of rescue workers transmitting a play-by-play through their body mikes is overshadowed by the looming, lugubrious presence of the Grim Reaper off to the side.)

Music serves as a powerful signal of emotion during various segments of the program, especially the assembly and the video shown at the assembly. Certain songs are popular choices year after year at schools across the country; the sentimental Sarah McLachlan tunes "I Will Remember You" and "Angel" are perennial favorites, as is Samuel Barber's haunting "Adagio for Strings" (the piece used in the climactic scenes of the well-known war movie *Platoon*). A California official surveying E15M programs around the state told me that music is a key element in setting the emotional tone of the assembly. "When you see a bunch of different programs you see the effect of having music," he said. "The kids were still talking in the crowd when the program began. Usually with the lights going down it gets quiet . . . but it needs music."

Another sensory cue, or marker, is conveyed through touch. The element of touch is often overlooked in studies of play frame; yet it is a powerful conduit for communication and meaning. Significant moments in the course of E15M are marked by gestures; the Grim Reaper's touch on a shoulder signals the "death" of the selected student, moving her into a realm separate from the staring classmates she leaves behind. When the Living Dead reunite with their parents and friends the next morning after the assembly, tearful hugs come with their "return to the living." One student posted this comment in September 2002 on the Every15Minutes.com Guestbook website: "After the morning ceremony when [the Living Dead student] was able to rejoin his classmates his friends all walked up just to touch him and establish that the day before was just a simulation."

Tears, too, can be considered a marker identifying frames within E15M. Tears can send the signal that a new emotional level or frame has been reached, and set off others; tears are curiously contagious. In almost every community, I observed or heard about the local high school football hero (or other big, strong male athlete) who broke down while reading his letter to his parents, setting off a torrent from his peers. Gary Ebersole has explored the concept of "tears-as-signs" (2000, 214); I discuss this idea further in chapter 4.

A Grim Reaper told me how his own tears had worked as a cue for a normally reserved student to release emotions. "All the girls were just sobbing, and there was this boy trying just to hold back—I had tears in my eyes too, I leaned forward, and I said, 'I'm the Grim Reaper, and if I can cry, you can cry.' And next thing you know, [*laughs*] he just kind of broke down and cried. Dabbing his eyes with Kleenex and things like that."

A role, in itself, is a kind of frame too, though more abstract than its clearly observable accoutrements. Folklorist Robert Lavenda, analyzing paradoxical frames in the context of community festivals, has commented on "the mystifying and perhaps troubling ambiguity and strangeness" in someone who simultaneously embodies both real-life and fantasy personae: "Participants are both characters and persons, deeply involved in the event but also constantly monitoring what is going on around them" (1991, 156, 166). Participants' ability to fulfill their roles appropriately can affect frame limits for themselves and for others, argues Jack Holcomb, who has studied Internet role-playing game communities where the smooth progress of play could be broken or compromised if some players became overimmersed in the game. This caused other members to become annoyed and mocking (2000, 72). I have not observed such a dynamic in Every 15 Minutes in cases where students exhibit extreme distress (uncontrolled sobbing, for example). Rather, apparent immersion in the simulated action has seemed to capture respectful interest from other students, who may well realize that the emotional reaction is based on more than the immediate game. One program organizer told me that almost everyone involved in her program "had an alcohol-related crash of a family friend or someone that they really cared about, and that's what makes it work. Because we can all relate to it, and so it's *believable.*" Testimonies such as hers confirm that scholars of play are not the only ones conscious of the ambiguous and embedded nature of frames; participants in this event have insight into their own and others' multilayered experiences.

Scholars of play often use frame analysis to try to organize the inherently messy world. Don Handelman, for example, asserts: "Boundaries are commonly marked by thresholds, whether these are thresholds of space (physical and visible), of time (counted and felt), or of sociality (known and normative) . . . they separate alternatives in an either/or fashion . . . These boundaries are constructs that retain their shape through either consensus or imposition" (1997, 40). But Sutton-Smith (1997) has challenged such black-and-white thinking, arguing that the distinction between play and not-play is difficult to draw, even when we can identify certain markers and boundaries. Boundaries that consist of self-referential paradox make life even more confusing. I noticed this in E15M as well. For example, administrators repeatedly refer to it as a "program" and as "reality" in the same breath; an organizer emphasized that "we're trying to make this as real as possible"; and kids are warned to "take this seriously—this is no game, it's reality!" Paradoxically, by these very conscious efforts and allusions, speakers remind everyone of the unreality of the scenario. In short, there would be no need to insist again and again how real it is if it *were* real.

Regardless of such exhortations, though, people can choose whether to take events seriously or dismiss them as "just play." Lavenda calls this "the subjunctive voice of play" (1991, 154). The stylized (or meta-communicative) nature of play actions identifies them as somehow different from everyday actions, though play enactments may be in close dialectical relationship with everyday reality, explains Sutton-Smith. "Play may be a paradox in communication terms (it is and it is not what it says it is), but play also involves maintaining the referential paradoxes throughout," he writes; a player must show "supreme awareness of the two levels of being, the virtual and the mundane, and how she can interact with both of them" (1997, 195–196).

AMBIGUITY—REAL VS. PRETEND, OR BOTH AT ONCE

Bateson, defining play, uses this metaphor: "The playful nip denotes the bite, but it does not denote what would be denoted by the bite" (1955, 41). Distinctions between pretend and real, between nip and bite, between "experience" and experience, have no straightforward or steadfast markers. Rather, each individual or collective experience comprises layer upon layer of reality and make-belief. Further, each experience can entail a range of real and imagined repercussions for participants. A media teacher who helped produce Every 15 Minutes near Los Angeles marveled: "That's the wonderful thing about a program like this: it saves you the angst and the pain of having to experience [a traumatic death] directly. As Benjamin Franklin said, 'Experience is a rough school, but a fool will learn by no other.'"

The educational value of "learning by experience" is thrown into a whirlpool of ambiguity by an activity like E15M, where "experience" takes on multiple meanings and takes place in multiple frames. When the territory that is mapped by the play frame is not clearly fictitious, as with tears, confusion arises easily. Even within an agreed-upon, deliberate play frame, elements of real and pretend are entwined, mixing and competing. Unexpected intrusions can cause "frame slippage," which Drewal calls "dangerous because it destabilizes a situation and throws it into a zone of ambiguity" (1992, 16).

Intentional actions within frames may denote real power relations; as a fictitious map, play reasserts the moral relationship among players, but ambiguously, contends Lindquist (2001, 6). The Living Dead, elevated to a new status in the Every 15 Minutes frame, still have a particular relationship to the adults directing the action. Within the slippery frames of the program, teenagers and adults alike negotiate, comment on, and play with the balance of power. Whether such slippage creates "dangerous" play is debatable. Could the ambiguity of the experience of trauma lead to negative consequences for some students, traumatize them? Certainly potential dangers lurk in the aftermath of E15M, but to follow individuals' psychic and behavioral changes is far beyond the scope of this book. What I present here are some examples of ambiguous play which, in my observations, did not endanger the life of the program itself.

As organizers prepare the Living Dead to begin their ordeal, they issue advice and predictions. "You guys are going to be on a bit of an emotional roller coaster, so if you feel a little overwhelmed by anything, let one of us know—there's plenty of counselors around," a California police coordinator told students. Students, in turn, self-consciously anticipate their own shock and distress. "They're going to make us cry!" one Living Dead girl said to another (with what I interpreted to be a tone more of curiosity than dread) as they rode the bus to the hotel for their retreat.

I often perceived a sense of jolliness about the instructions given to role-players as the stage was set for the mock accident. A Maryland police officer, coaching a boy for his role as a bicyclist who gets killed by the crash, described the planned sequence of events and added, "Have you ever died before?" They both laughed. A teacher at another school looked forward to playing dead in the accident scene. "I think my entire junior class is going to stand up and cheer!" he said with amusement. "They have a research paper due, and they're going to be like 'Yeah, no papers, who's gonna grade it!'" A parent volunteer in Los Angeles remarked on what a good time she was having with the other mothers in the makeup room; she told me that her friend was excited "to get herself in the mood for the death notification" she would receive later that day. A student chosen for his intimidating stature to play the Grim Reaper repeated, "Off with their heads! Off with their heads!" in a high falsetto, pausing to declare that there was "nothing a good Christian wants better than to be Death!"

Ambiguity pervades this process, not only in the notion of staged tragedy but in the conceptions of how "dead" people ought to look and behave within it. In an interview, the police coordinator from a Texas town explained that his "Living Dead went back to class because of Texas [attendance] rules, but they couldn't talk, even to teachers. They were *dead*, they were just sitting in the back . . . They would not sit in their regular assigned seat, but somewhere else, to try to give the effect that 'I'm not here.'" Face paint on the Living Dead, insisted an administrator in New Mexico, "makes it more real. If you just leave them plain, like okay, you know, it's just a plain person sitting there."

Participants come to their roles with varying assumptions about appropriate conduct, often expressed with a sense of irony or humor. "Don't laugh—you are Death! You are not allowed to laugh!" a Maryland police officer commanded the Grim Reaper with exaggerated solemnity; his colleague jokingly reprimanded the recently reaped students, "No smiling when you're dead!" A Southern California student protested, "Dead people don't do homework" when adults suggested the group in the "holding room" pass the time by studying. "I don't think dead people should be having so much fun," mused the daughter of a parent organizer, too young to participate in the program but observing the snacks and shenanigans in the holding room.

The Living Dead's communications exemplify ambiguity both outwardly and internally. In a small Indiana town, one "crash victim" recalled: "I couldn't see anything, but I could hear beer cans rolling around and the drunk driver murmuring, the police and helicopter and sirens. When they opened the cars you could hear the Jaws of Life, you could hear them prying the stuff open. It was scary, I didn't know if it would hurt me—if you're dead you're not supposed to feel it." Within E15M's fluid layers of frames, even normally straightforward sensations may sway under the influence of ambiguity. An assistant principal in California related an example of this effect. "We had this student transported to [the hospital], and she's pronounced dead. And the mother came in to identify the body. But the mother didn't know that they had soaked the daughter's hand in ice, to make it cold, and so when she went to go touch her hand, her hand was—you know!" He shuddered; I asked whether the hand would really be that cold on an actual dead body, and he replied, "It wouldn't be *that* cold, but it was—it was a shock for her—so that was the one experience that really made it very real."

Even when we recognize a frame, writes Roger Abrahams (1986), we may struggle to determine whether play is really taking place, especially "when actors play a part that carries a social or political message with which they have been identified off-stage." He alludes to "situations of deep play, where the intensity, the investment in the exchange, the degree of focus, and the representative symbolic character of the activity are so profound that it is often difficult to draw the line between 'just play' and deep seriousness" (29–30). Participants clearly suffer genuine emotions, including fear, as they go through motions they understand to be staged. Many recount such ambiguous moments. A counselor in Maryland, describing the parental death notifications, remarked, "It's amazing, the parents cry even though they know what's happening—they want to be reassured. They cry and say, 'This is that program, isn't it?' Even though they know in advance. It's the drama of it that hits you—really wild!" Later on, at the retreat, the "drunk driver" from this school attested to her own sensations of fear: "I was shaking the whole day! People were saying, 'Why are you so scared, why are you scared?' I couldn't answer, but now I know—it's because it was *so* real." The counselor validated the student's comment: "Sometimes you can't separate the reality of the feeling from the scene."

Organizers may try to manage and prepare for overflows of such emotion. "I don't want you to get upset about sitting in the police station in the cell for a while," a policewoman advised one drunk driver. "The officers are really nice and everything, you know, if you need anything to drink or anything, just let them know. But I'm just letting you know that you might be sitting there for a while, okay? In a cell. So don't panic. Okay?"

Addressing their audience at the concluding assembly, the Living Dead relate their emotional journeys. One role-player spoke of the guilt and anxiety the crash scene had triggered for him:

> I told myself from the beginning, this isn't going to be a big deal, I'm just *pretending* that I'm drunk, I'm just pretending that I killed my friend and a teacher. And then when I sat in the car yesterday to get ready for everyone to come out, and I saw the whole school run out, and all the smoke, and then the cop comes up to the car, and he's yelling at me, all I wanted was to find out where [my friend] was, and they wouldn't let me know, and that's like my best friend, and all of a sudden everything felt real. I felt like I was responsible for everything that had just happened, and they wouldn't let me find out where anyone was and they wouldn't let me out of the car. Then I got out in front of everybody, and they wouldn't let me turn around and I couldn't move or see what was going on, and I was so nervous and scared, I was shaking. A

lot of people told me that I acted really good yesterday, and it looked real. That's 'cause it *was* real.

The blurring of simulated and authentic feeling is a typical phenomenon among the role-players in E15M, and it is acknowledged and supported by the interactions of participants—in their warnings, words of comfort, and confessions. "There is much ambiguity in the adult-child relationship about fantasy," points out Sutton-Smith; "At the same time, imaginative activity is itself often extremely ambiguous as to what it expresses, what it conceals, and what on earth it means" (1997, 172).

In Maryland, I stood with a member of Students against Drunk Driving, watching a group of senior girls, spectators in the front row at the crash scene. The girls clung to each other and wept. "For some of them maybe it's real, for some of them it's definitely show," said the student next to me. "You've got to kind of know the person to be able to tell."

THE METAPHOR THAT IS MEANT

Bateson has attempted to draw a distinction between messages that are "mood-signs" and "messages that simulate mood-signs (in play, threat, histrionics, etc.)"; he also refers to a third type of message enabling us to discriminate between the mood-signs and the simulated mood-signs (1955, 49). The pure mood-signs common in E15M include pounding hearts, trembling, tears, and a range of subjectively authentic emotions that can be triggered by the symbolic scenario. Given the tenacious ambiguity of the mock tragedy in Every 15 Minutes, including its shifting markers, Bateson's phrase "the metaphor that is meant" is particularly useful. He presents this concept to explain "the flag which men will die to save . . . an attempt to deny the difference between map and territory, and to get back to the absolute innocence of communication by means of pure mood-signs" (43). This is not unlike the effect Bateson describes wherein "a man experiences the full intensity of subjective terror when a spear is flung at him out of a 3-D screen or when he falls headlong from some peak created in his own mind in the intensity of nightmare . . . the images did not denote that which they seemed to denote, but these images did really evoke that terror which would have been evoked by a real spear or a real precipice" (44).

The ordeal of the Living Dead and their parents, though its gravity is imagined, can evoke strong sentiments and provoke literal actions. One "bereaved" mother was eager to talk about the difficulty of the overnight separation from her son: "At 3:00 in the morning I got up and crawled in his bed to see if I could smell him! And I slept in his bed. And I broke down then. It was terrible!" Imagining an irreversible loss is potentially quite painful, as a mother in New Mexico reflected: "I understand now why they made them spend the night away from home—representing that absence away from home was what made the impact. They're away from home on other occasions, but we always know they're coming home. So what happens if they *don't* come back?"

A parent interviewed by her local newspaper in Maryland described the urge to actively respond to the make-believe situation: "When I first saw him just laying there [in the emergency room] I wanted to shake him and say, 'What did I tell you about drinking and driving?' . . . It seems so real. I was a nervous wreck the entire morning" (Pope 2000). In that community, a parent who spoke at the assembly recalled undeniable pain and frustration:

> I experienced the loss of [my son] because when he was calling us from jail, I asked if we could come and see him and he said no. I wanted to talk to him, and somebody told him that he had to get off the phone. When I did hang up, I was really angry [*speaking through tears*] that somebody else was telling me that I couldn't see my son. To see him in that court scene, to know that he was going to have to spend time in prison, because of the result of his actions and his choices that he made, somebody would be telling me that I couldn't see him, that he couldn't come home and he couldn't be with us. And he couldn't be part of our family on a daily basis. That's a loss. And I grieved over that loss yesterday, and it bothered me all day, because he wasn't home, where he belongs, with us. There's no way to describe how painful that was.

"It was chilling to hear the letters," a counselor told me after the assembly. "I just sobbed in the back of the auditorium. I know and like these people, and I can just picture the agony and anguish they were going through as they were writing these letters."

In comments of participants of all sorts, examples of Bateson's "metaphor that is meant" abound. One teacher demonstrated her emotion to each student pulled from her classroom by the Grim Reaper: "I hugged each one of them and told them that I would truly miss them, and then I told them one special thing about themselves that I would miss." "It's hard to imagine the impact until you've experienced it," said a Living Dead girl, then started to sob at the assembly podium as she told her audience how "during the accident my dad came up to me and gave me a hug and he started crying, and my father isn't one to cry . . ." Even more visceral was the effect described to me by a principal's secretary, who said that a student took one look at the crash scene and fainted into her arms. For her, this evidence represented E15M's emotional power: "He was just so overcome by what he saw."

These types of experiences exemplify what Csikszentmihalyi (1975) has called "flow." The psychologist defines flow as a state in which the ego is temporarily superseded by immersion in the activity of play, and actions follow upon each other with no apparent conscious effort by the actor, who "experiences it as a unified flowing from one moment to the next, in which he is in control of his actions, and in which there is little distinction between self and environment, between stimulus and response, or between past, present, and future" (36). Moments of flow, perhaps, are contributing to the experience of participants who find themselves caught up in surprisingly strong emotional currents, metaphor and reality streaming together with ambiguous meaning.

ADDING A LITTLE REALITY

Every 15 Minutes is commonly promoted as a way to achieve two goals at once—shaking up teenagers who "think they are immortal" and providing a training drill for the emergency personnel. Simulations of real-life activities may be rehearsals that serve various purposes. Goffman (1974) cites the use of manikins in medical education as "practicings" (59) that provide lifelike experience in performing the procedures students need to master. "Demonstrations," or how-to exhibitions and warnings, can have "embarrassing ambiguities" (68), he observes. "Although the demonstrating of something can be radically different from the doing of that something, there is still some carry-over—especially if 'real' equipment is used" (67). The facilitators of E15M's mock traumatic scenes rely heavily on special effects, costuming, and theatrics. They design these cautionary demonstrations to include numerous professional and personal touches, all intended to make the proceedings feel more real. But hitting just the right dramatic tone is not easy, one policeman pointed out, remembering an instance that certainly qualifies as an embarrassing ambiguity. "We tell [the drunk driver] to resist a little when he gets arrested, but last year he did a little too much and officers slammed him on the hood of the car. 'Next year,' we said, 'resist, but not too much!'"

"I ended up writing all the obituaries," said a media tech teacher who produced E15M at a school outside of Washington, DC. "Kids were writing them and handing them in, and I thought, 'These don't sound like obituaries.' I had to retype them, so as I was doing it I beefed them up—said when the accident happened, what funeral home they're at, etc.—to add a little reality." In one of the California schools that I observed, counselors wrote the Living Dead students' obituaries, reasoning that if the parents did it, they would appear to be "planning their kids' death . . . and you don't plan, when they're in an accident." (The inherent paradox of this explanation is apparent, as parents are prepped for months to endure their children's simulated death, with meticulous planning by everyone involved.) In yet another example of paradoxical and unstable frames of real and pretend, one student posted this message on the Every15Minutes.com Guestbook site in February 2002: "This is an amazing program, with an even more amazing message behind it. I have a younger brother attending one of the E15M schools and I would like to thank you for letting in a little bit of reality into his otherwise fake existence."

Organizers compliment each other's creativity, admire the gruesome masterpieces of the makeup artists, and critique the staging of scenes such as the drunk driver's trip to jail. "They did a *really* nice job with clanging that metal door shut" on him, a counselor remarked approvingly. Planning committees sometimes argue for months over the likely effectiveness of specific symbols or activities. Two neighboring New Mexico schools staged their mock funerals only after agonizing debate, according to a program coordinator: "We considered using the mirror—where the kids will file by an open coffin and there's a mirror placed in there where they see a reflection of themselves. We considered it, and both schools have decided, 'Not yet.'" She broke into peals of laughter, and continued: "It's too much—it would startle too many people, or maybe make it a *funny* thing, you know, rather than a *real* thing." Later, explaining to me why she required every member of the Living Dead to have at least one parent involved in the program, she sounded the same theme. "The parent has to be involved. It's too much for a child to go through on their own—and, that's not real. See, we're trying to make this as real as possible: somebody from the family has to be involved."

One high school featured photos of its E15M program, along with a description referring to "the overwhelming power of love and grief," on its official website. "The fact that it was just imagined grief should serve as powerful warning. Real drunk-driving accidents aren't imaginary and don't end after two days. The dead write no letters; survivors have no one to read them to." Despite this standard acknowledgment of the event's contrived nature, the actions that take place during these two days imply differently. "The more you make it look real, the more realistic people will *act,*" a local Air Force disaster-drill specialist (recruited by the school for his makeup expertise) told me. He carefully placed a plastic severed hand near a "victim" who lay prone by the accident scene. Then he busied himself setting up burning canisters to create billows of smoke around the wreckage.

MEDIA ADDS ANOTHER LAYER

"If it bleeds, it leads," as the saying goes about the media's appetite for violent material. Predictably, reporters descend on Every 15 Minutes to capture its colorful action. Observing the choices of print and photojournalists, I saw them consistently gravitating toward the visibly emotional students in the crowd. Most of the resulting news reports resemble each other, quoting and repeating standard refrains (such as "If one life is saved it's all worth it" and, of course, the erroneous title statistic).

More intriguing, however, is the ambiguity between fact and fiction that frequently seeps into the news reports. Driving to an Every 15 Minutes event at one school in New Mexico early one morning, I was struck by the local radio deejay's announcement (without a hint of irony): "This morning, twenty teenagers will die at [the local] High School." Television reports open with a similarly credulous tone, and tend to slip into literal voice, echoing the program participants' blend of real and pretend. "Because this is a simulation, the judge doesn't have to worry about due process," a *Today Show* correspondent informed viewers in an April 2001 segment, and went on: "In a couple of minutes, Derek is found guilty and sentenced on the spot, forty-five years to life."

"Students at [the local] High School learned what a person's brain looks like splattered on the ground this morning," began the front-page story in one Idaho newspaper (Hedland 1994). Some newspapers publish the Living Dead obituaries, and local cable access stations may broadcast these obituaries or the school-produced video first shown at the school assembly. This widens the frame of the program, extending its reach to more community members who can collaborate in the pretense.

Many program administrators have expressed to me their conviction that incorporating the media attention into the scenario can't hurt—that it in fact adds to the desired ambiance and lends authenticity to the reenactment. Therefore they allow the media to fill, within the play frame, the role that it occupies also in real life. This brings journalists in to participate in a manner comparable to the emergency rescue workers and law-enforcement personnel, yet with even more layers of embedded frames. That is, the media play themselves covering the story while simultaneously they cover the same events for a differently framed story. (Regardless of frame, most of the stories adopt a similar saddened and alarmed tone.) The three senior girls crying in the front row, mentioned earlier in this chapter, were eager to be interviewed by a local newspaper correspondent. The narrative published the next day implied stark tragedy, describing the student as crying while she watched one of her close friends being zipped into a body bag and another laid on a stretcher after the drunk driver of the Ford Escort they were riding in hit a bicyclist and a tree in the school's parking lot.

An organizer gave me her enthusiastic endorsement of this media presence. "We've got all these cameras out—and that's why it becomes more *real!* See, the hype! These kids are seeing cameras everywhere, they're seeing the media . . . I mean, the minute there's an accident, how many cameras do you have there? If there's a big tragic event, who's there? The media!"

Whether or not they make it onto the evening news, students and adults are glad to get some recognition for their efforts, and the flashbulbs and interviews fit right in with the action. Some schools, nervous that local stations might neglect to send correspondents, take the initiative and ask a local media representative to act like a "live-action reporter" with a microphone at the scene, interviewing people for an imaginary feature.

As these examples demonstrate, play activity can be embedded within the outer frame of a literal situation, and the relationships and boundaries become even more bewildering when we consider the media element coloring E15M's overlapping sets. Susan Hoyle noted a similar thing in her 1993 analysis of boys playing at sportscasting: The boys "shift between speaking as a sportscaster, in which capacity they report the events of the game, and speaking as themselves, in which capacity they seek to resolve procedural difficulties and keep the game going . . . They shift away from announcing the action . . . to act out 'interviews with a player' . . . embedding one nonliteral participation framework within another" (116). In addition, "the footing of the literal situation [interrupting for arguments, questions, and interferences] is embedded within the footing of the sportscast" (125).

STEPPING IN AND OUT OF THE FRAME

"When the play frame edges too close to not-play, the play is over," proposes Lavenda (1992, 23). But, at least in the case of Every 15 Minutes, frames may be less fragile and more malleable than Lavenda implies. The following anecdotes from my firsthand research exemplify the natural stepping in and out of frame that occurs during every stage of this intricate phenomenon.

In general, a policeman in uniform has the duty of following each "reaping" by reading the obituary of the "dead" student to the class. Planners envision this as a somber moment, but in fact the mood may fluctuate easily, dependent on factors such as the dynamics already present in that classroom, the social status of the chosen student, and the sense of authority conveyed (or not) by the cop. One California police coordinator instructed officers in advance, "After you're done reading the obituaries you may ask if the kids have any questions about the DUI process, what happens from a law-enforcement standpoint . . . Most of the kids are pretty shocked. They don't say a whole lot. Some will kind of act a little goofy. Some nervous laughter, if you will. But for the most part, anything that they may ask about getting arrested for DUI or what have you—that's what you're there for." Though most obituary readings do not allow question-and-answer opportunities, this case illustrates the ease with which people can switch gears, from the tense simulation of a death announcement to the more casual back-and-forth of familiar relationships. In fact, an officer I followed on his obituary rounds at this school found himself peppered with queries regarding what constitutional rights protect teenagers against having their cars searched or their parties broken up. With this addendum to the obituaries, the classroom's atmosphere changed quickly and noticeably, becoming animated as students seized the chance to interact with a police officer outside the normal frame (in which he might issue a citation at any moment).

In another school, I witnessed an officer in full formal dress uniform delivering an obituary, his manner deadpan. After he left the room, students immediately began to discuss the taps on the soles of his shoes. Their teacher joined in with the comment: "If it were a happier occasion, maybe he'd do a tap dance for us, but seeing as it's such a heavy, sad occasion . . . "

In the holding room, the role-players and Living Dead get their faces made up, gorge on great quantities of junk food, and wait in anticipation (and often apprehension) for the emotional roller coaster ride they have been warned to expect from their tour and retreat. This holding room (or prep room) marks an in-between realm, where the students have just "died" yet are allowed to interact normally with other Living Dead and are attended to by a bevy of solicitous parent volunteers. Here, some players hopscotch lightly between frames of play and ordinary life. In an interaction that took place at a Maryland school before the mock accident but between reapings, the Grim Reaper, a local youth mentor, coached the boy who would play the part of the driver on how to act drunk. The Reaper stood with his hood thrown back over his shoulders, manipulating a slice of pizza in one hand and gesturing with the other. He told the student how to stand on one leg and hop around as though he were being given a sobriety test, how to appear off balance, and how to act as though he didn't understand what the officer was saying or what was going on—"That'll add more realism to it." His protégé, casual in a New York Knicks jersey and unlaced basketball shoes, smiled and nodded attentively, clearly on good terms already with the Reaper.

In a different program, a parent who had volunteered to escort the reaped students to the makeup room came up with his own innovation to enhance their transition into a new frame: he gave each one a talk on how he was taking them across the river Styx.

> That was just off the top of my head! It's just that when you die, it's the loneliest journey anyone will ever take, but they wanted us to escort the kids over to the makeup room. So in a way, it was not really realistic. So I just wanted them to start thinking of themselves as being dead. Thinking of themselves being in the past . . . Some of them as we started to walk over were just sort of elated they got out of class. I mean, they knew it was a serious experience, but the class had reacted with laughter or something, so they needed to rethink at that moment and start thinking about the experience that they were going to be going through. I would say, "You *were* so-and-so," and I'd get this reaction, like suddenly they realized that they were no longer [alive].

A girl who had just received this mythology-themed escort described her perceptions. "When he was talking about it, I could picture myself walking across there by myself," she said. "I was thinking about it, like, gosh, I could have done a lot of things." I asked her if she was thinking of herself in the past tense at that moment; "Yeah. I am," she said.

Once across the river Styx, however, the Living Dead at this school were by no means stuck in the past tense. In their holding room, amid mountains of pizza and soda, they sprawled on couches, some in each other's arms, flirting, teasing, and wrestling. Half the girls removed their black Living Dead T-shirts in favor of their tight tank tops showing cleavage on top of short shorts and miniskirts. The boys burped loudly; the girls reacted with *ewwww*s of disgust; the student playing the Grim Reaper popped his video of *Jaws* into the VCR, and the group watched with shrieks of hilarity. "How can you guys *laugh?*" wondered the dean in charge of the program.

The dean's question may have no conclusive answer. Much of the time, we don't know exactly why we are laughing, why we are crying, or what carries us back and forth across the river between these responses. Anyone who attempts to map such treacherous journeys and their emergent emotions attempts a truly Sisyphean task. The porous nature of the E15M event brings these issues into striking relief.

In and Out of Frame: The Crash

"It makes my mind boggle—one minute you're like, 'Oh, yeah, I'm just doing a program,' but sitting there in the car and getting people pulled out around you, all of a sudden, it's crazy," said a student about his view from the "drunk driver" seat in a Maryland E15M crash. In an instant, participants may find themselves switching from matter-of-factly filling assigned roles to expanding in them. Another role-player explained to her classmates at the retreat:

> In the car we were joking and laughing, and tasting the fake blood on the door. Then the fireman comes in and wakes me up, and I open my eyes and see [another student victim] moaning in pain, and then I was screaming, and getting pulled out [of the car]—everything was so real. I was like yelling at the cop and cursing at him, and I had tears running down my face because it hit me so hard. Everyone was acting like it was really real. When I was sitting in the car and he finally took off the handcuffs, I took a deep breath, and I was like, "I can't believe that was fake."

A parent whom I contacted through her posting on the Every 15 Minutes Guestbook website related her experience in personal correspondence: "My daughter was one of the victims. She suffered neck injuries, facial abrasions and a broken leg. Even though I had applied her make-up and we had all been joking and laughing beforehand, when the action began and she started screaming, 'I want my mom! I can't move, where's my mom!' the tears just rolled out of my eyes. It was frightening and heartbreaking."

Adults have expressed surprise at their own strong reactions, even while taking the simulated events in stride. The media technology teacher who taped the hospital death scene for his school's video documentary told me later about the impression the task made on him: "[The student playing the victim] didn't move, he was the greatest. [*Laughs*] I just thought it was great! Finally when we said, 'Cut,' he just sat up and said, 'Hi!' [*Laughs*] But [earlier,] after he had been declared dead, I heard one of the nurses who was still playing her role say, 'What a waste.' And I started to cry. It just blew me away. He was lying there dead still. It was quite an experience."

A parent in a Los Angeles suburb cheerfully commented on the number of passersby stopping to watch the crash scene (many with their young children in tow): "The more it gets out, these people could know some people in another city and tell them and *they* could do this program . . . It's a domino effect. I know our Rotary Club wants to make this an international program, and so does our Optimist Club!" But in the next instant her eyes filled with tears at the sight of her regular babysitter walking by wearing Living Dead face paint. "This is so hard," she confided. "I've known these kids for so long, it's just so hard!"

The dramatic frame can fade as quickly as it takes shape, and the attention of the spectators at the accident is particularly tenuous. Adults as well as students bring a critical consciousness and a lively commentary to the proceedings, as well as an awareness of others' perspectives. One parent told me: "I was at the accident last time, and it probably went on, you know, for the twenty-five minutes that the lunch period lasted, and I think it was too long . . . It started getting funny, for some of [the students]. You know: [*imitates mocking student voice*] 'Oh, look at so-and-so, he's not moving! Let's see if we can make him!' You know? It lost its impact! Certainly there are some kids who were still very much wrapped up in it, but there were a lot of kids that were out there just to be out of school."

Frame shifts can be deliberate, sudden, or extremely subtle. And participants' steps in and out of frame, if we were to trace them, would lead through both public and personal space, both past and present time. One parent acknowledged that the presence of the cameraman as the doctor delivered the news of her son's "death" colored her experience at the hospital. "It was a tiny room, and I felt he was very close to us, and all I saw was that metal box [the camera] in the corner of my eye—I did and I didn't see it." Another mother who watched her daughter "flatline" told me she had flashbacks to her sister's death years ago, which made her particularly emotional during the scene.

In and Out of Frame: On Retreat

In the extraordinary setting of the retreat, separate from the everyday social hierarchies of their high school, students are encouraged to talk about personal struggles in discussion activities with the rest of the Living Dead group. After a few of them have opened up, the self-revelations tend to fly thick and fast, and students often comment that previous divisions between popular and unpopular groups have melted away. They also express a hypothetical intention to keep those divisions and inhibitions from reappearing—vowing to tell their friends how much they love them every day, and to stop ignoring people outside their social clique. Students often repeat such resolutions in the letters they read before the assembly the next day; whether they keep them, or for how long, may constitute a topic for further study.

Counselors and administrators at the retreat support these new interpretations and conventions of communication, but not without stepping in and out of frame as quickly and casually as their teenage charges do. (Sometimes these incongruities themselves are framed as therapeutic: time in the hot tub at the hotel is "necessary decompression time," white teddy bears were distributed to one group for reassurance, and one Ohio contingent went to the movies to see *Spiderman* before writing their letters from the grave.) "Don't take this lightly," an assistant principal scolded the Living Dead at a retreat outside of Washington, DC; he then advised them that their participation in the program was going to look great on their résumés. The police coordinator of a nearby school's program warned her group, as they wrote their letters to read at the next day's assembly, "Don't express anything you might not want the media to hear—think about who you might be later in life." Her remark was frame breaking; within the E15M frame generally, much is revealed that would be concealed in normal life. The coordinator was likely implying that a run for office later in life would be jeopardized by too much confessional detail now, and yet the Living Dead are supposed to behave and think under the pretense that their futures are wiped out. The paradox of writing a public letter that must begin, "If I had only had the chance to tell you . . . " while keeping a potential political career in the back of one's mind underscores just how tangled the many frames of E15M can get.

One Southern California counselor spoke of her strategy for setting the right mood at the retreat: "I tried very hard to always speak in the past tense. The other counselors and I made a conscious effort to say 'was' and 'were.'

The idea is that you're in a suspended reality. If I was going to sit and make jokes about it, which was really tempting at times, I would have gone, '*doo doo doo doo doo doo doo doo*! [tune of the *Twilight Zone* theme song]' You know?" She laughed. In real life, it may be hard to keep the focus on death, no matter how well one plans the mock funeral.

In and Out of Frame: Onstage

The context of the public stage showcases some dramatic shifts in frame. Every 15 Minutes assemblies already have a structure that combines and alternates frames of fiction and reality, as guest speakers with harrowing stories of personal loss share the program agenda with E15M role-players. (The latter invariably show more visible emotion than the former; as volunteers for "tragedy," their attraction to the performance aspect, and the newness of their experience, may contribute to this disparity.) "At our assembly, kids read a letter what their life would have been if they hadn't died," said the police chief from a small city in Texas. "Then the last thing we do is we have anyone who's been touched by a DWI come forward, and about fifty people will come down [onstage]." Assembly programs incorporate and juxtapose elements with a vast range of tones, from slides of actual accident scenes (reminiscent of the driver's education scare tactics mentioned in chapter 2) to political-themed speeches by local government representatives, musical numbers by student bands, and displays of the Living Dead's portraits enlarged and posted on easels.

Shifts below the staged surface have visible signs as well. At one school's E15M assembly, students who had expressed hilarity throughout the two-day event suddenly dissolved into tears when they found themselves standing at the podium facing a spotlight and microphone. At another school, the Living Dead rehearsed their speeches stoically into the microphone in the empty auditorium, but then broke down an hour later when the student body was there to hear them. And, during the course of a single speech, a speaker as well as her audience can easily change footing (Goffman's term for attitude or stance within a frame). A crash victim role-player in Los Angeles inserted joking comments throughout his address—lying on the gravel "was hot, and I wanted to put sunscreen on my face but I had no hand," he said, to appreciative giggles from the crowd. But reaching the part of his narration where "they put me on a gurney to go in the ambulance," he broke abruptly into tears, inspiring his fellow Living Dead members to call out encouragement ("Come on, Kevin, keep it up!") from their seats behind him on the stage.

Such shifts may influence and be influenced by others, as frames overlap in public interaction. According to a New Mexico organizer, parents designated as assembly speakers "will ask us, 'What do you want us to say?' They kind of want us to script it, and we say no, this is something *you* have to do. And so they're a little lost with it, but it's incredible because once they start hearing everybody else talking about it, they just get up there and just do it . . . and the things that come out! I don't think some of them even planned to have this much come out!"

PLAYFULNESS AND THE LIVING DEAD

Brian Sutton-Smith has suggested that while *play* can be contained by frames surrounding specific activities, *playfulness* is disruptive of frames (1997, 196). Playfulness has been characterized as "an attitude toward conducting any and all activities, where agents disrupt routines, manipulate the expected, and even play with the accepted frames of play itself" (Lindquist 2001). Bateson, in analyzing childhood behavior, has stated that "such combinations as histrionic play, bluff, playful threat, and so on form together a single total complex of phenomena," and that "not only histrionics but spectatorship," as well as self-pity, should also be included in this complex (1955, 42). Some scholars of play have approached playfulness gingerly. "Playfulness is a volatile, sometimes dangerously explosive essence, which cultural institutions seek to bottle or contain . . . in modes of simulation such as theater, and in controlled disorientation, from roller coasters to dervish dancing," writes renowned ritual scholar Victor Turner (1983, 233).

But playful frame breaking has been a fertile area for scholarly research. Margaret Drewal, in her investigation of Yoruba play and ritual in Nigeria, uses the term *improvisation* to refer to "a whole gamut of spontaneous individual moves: ruses, parodies, transpositions, recontextualizations, elaborations, condensations, interruptions, interventions, and more." These elements, though "destabilizing," are normal and expected, Drewal asserts; innovations "do not break with tradition but rather are continuations of it in the spirit of improvisation" (1992, 20).

Rules "are much more open for debate than is commonly reported in the literature," points out Goodwin. "Although rules for coordinating jump rope activity are highly patterned, the ways in which any particular game is played are open for negotiation on each occasion of its performance, not only prior to the game but also during its course" (1985, 316). Goodwin documents participants' comments on others' activity, interruptions to rhyme recitations, criticisms, corrections, and rule changes; she notes that these breaks are "not treated as interruptive but rather as appropriate" (320). Within the frame of play, participants negotiate and "continue disputes that typify their everyday interaction" (326).

Even within the contained simulation and controlled disorientation of E15M's "emotional roller coaster," playfulness rears its volatile head, as I witnessed while accompanying the Living Dead on their journey beyond their urban high school east of Los Angeles. Chaperoned by the female dean who implemented the program, the students were to experience a trial, booking at the police station, and "identity-building" activities led by a youth outreach group called Friday Night Live. Throughout the afternoon and evening, the participants played with multiple frames, with such high-spirited abandon that I found their footings a challenge to follow.

The group members were taken to a district courthouse to watch their classmate go through a mock trial in her role as the drunk driver. She sat at the witness stand, chewing gum and wearing a black T-shirt—not the uniform shirt of the Living Dead, but her own—with the word *Ambiguous* printed on the front. (This seemed a striking, if unintended, parallel.) A private attorney donating his time to the program played her defense lawyer, and asked several inarticulate questions. The public prosecutor gave a dramatic speech, hamming up his anti-DUI lecture before the blank-faced audience of the Living Dead (and a bewildered tour group of Chinese bureaucrats who were visiting the courthouse to see the American justice system in action). The "drunk driver" lost her composure at one point: she started to cry when her lawyer asked if she had been fighting with the friends who were killed in the crash, but then she wiped her eyes and recovered quickly.

The group was then bused to the police station for a tour of the jail, guided by an officer who appeared intent on coming across as "cool" to the kids. An alumnus of their own high school, he told them stories about his former baseball team's tough reputation, bragging about how they had lost every game but won every fight. Shifting tone momentarily, he sternly told them their school had a better reputation now than it used to, and that they shouldn't "ruin it by screwing around" in the police station. He then launched into anecdotes about rich people and celebrities who paid $85 a night to stay at the station's jail, more private and safe than the regular prison. Adults and students alike made numerous jokes about prison rape (also mentioned earlier outside the courtroom by a sheriff who apparently intended it as a threat to scare the kids out of ending up in jail). The group heard details about what inmates have to wear, including the jock strap they are issued for underwear—at this, the dean directing the program screeched with laughter: "They get a *floss!*" The friendly cop guiding the tour continued to offer entertaining details, including how "when you shoot someone they keep coming at you like a chicken with its head cut off."

Afterward, outside the police station, the students waited for their chartered bus, horsing around on the lawn in the shade of a big tree. They smiled and flexed their muscles as the dean posed them for group photos, passed around pictures from the previous weekend's senior prom, complained about the restaurant chosen for dinner that night, and demanded to know whether they would have time to swim at the hotel. Several girls took off their black Living Dead T-shirts, preferring their tiny tank tops and shorts. The dean did not object to this subversion of the rules, although she tried to coax the "drunk driver" into wearing her Living Dead shirt for a souvenir photo: "Come on! Put it on—you're the *star!*"

Students and administrators argued over whether they should film a scene (for the video to be shown at the assembly) with the drunk driver calling her mother from jail. The girl protested that her mom had probably forgotten about the program and would "freak out," thinking the phone call was real, but the dean brushed off her objections: "Didn't you tell your mom about this?! Oh, just do it! She'll be *fine!*" This program organizer, in my observation, continually alternated between two equally raucous registers: joking, or barking at people to get in line. She teased students knowingly about who would be sneaking into whose room during the night at the hotel, but in the next breath, she warned students she would call their parents to pick them up if she found them "screwing around" with each other, ordering room service, or trashing the place. When a fellow chaperone seemed upset at the rowdiness of the Living Dead, the dean told me, "She needs to lighten up! They need to have some fun—they're kids! They need to have some downtime."

The boisterous atmosphere persisted through the retreat activities, which included games of hacky sack, Twister, and remembering names. Two Living Dead boys left for their rooms early; the Friday Night Live leader assessed the mood of the group in general as "punchy and unfocused." He seemed unconcerned, though, telling me he had to get home in time to watch *Friends* (a hit television sitcom) or else "there's going to be a real problem." Another chaperone expressed annoyance with the lack of control, and tried to revive a more serious ambiance as she announced the start of the letter-writing phase. "Write something from your heart to your parents," she said tersely.

The dean, arguing playfully with the students about how long they could stay in the pool and about the next morning's wake-up call, continued to jump back and forth between joining in the kids' irreverent hilarity and barking out orders. Under her inconsistent style of authority, it was unclear whether any of E15M's standard rules or principles held importance for her. Disregarding the "no contact" rule, she urged the Living Dead to call their parents from the hotel pay phone and make sure they were coming to the assembly. I perceived the dean's energy as focused on getting through the program—which she told me she had brought to the school despite resistance from skeptical higher-ups, from the local Asian immigrant community whose cultural values were offended by the death play, and from "stupid kids." I noticed her mugging, wisecracking, and hamming it up at every step during the event. Why would she go to all this trouble to set up E15M's frame, only to constantly interrupt it? I could only guess at her motivations, but I did wonder if there was any significance to an off-the-cuff comment she made at the hotel while reminding the kids, writing their letters to their parents, that they had better take this seriously. "My mom was an alcoholic, she left our family when I was twelve," she announced suddenly, before going back to teasing about which boys and girls might have romantic trysts, and whose parents she was going to call if they ordered pay-per-view.

The next morning, the Living Dead were rehearsed for their assembly, with cheerleading from the dean: "Let's have a little spirit here! This is *spiritual!*" In preparing for this performance, the most public stage of the program, the dean attempted to rein in the kids' playfulness, yet still occasionally engaged in her own antics. She coached them on their processional with candles, and on their handling of the casket that would be carried into the gymnasium by the Grim Reaper and four pallbearers. "Set it down! Lift it up again! Set it *down!* Guys, this is going to be embarrassing! There's going to be 1,000 people, like parents and everything, can we just be, like, serious, for a while? When you go to a funeral, do people just kind of walk out with the casket? [*imitating clownish gait*] Maybe Montana would like to get in the coffin and be a weight in there!" (I declined.)

After the previous twenty-four hours of manipulations, improvisations, parody, subversions, and unlimited other frame breaks, it was remarkable to

witness the flood of tears unleashed from these Living Dead when their shin-
ing moment arrived. A malfunctioning sound system made their speeches
mostly indecipherable, but the teenagers displayed striking emotional affect.
They sat in folding chairs before the packed bleachers in the gym, their
parents (the ones who showed up, for many did not) in rows of chairs facing them. Each parent who spoke laid a bouquet of flowers on the coffin.
Boxes of Kleenex were passed up and down the rows. The dean watched the
drama's conclusion with an expression of satisfaction and relief, remarking
how effective the candles were in setting the mood. She told me that it was
a good thing she hadn't checked the candles out with the principal before
the assembly: "He never would have let me have them walk into the gym
with them lit."

SLIPPERY STEPS, AMBIGUOUS ACTS

"Play acts often serve multiple, contradictory purposes simultaneously," notes Richard Schechner in an essay on the ways people use play
and negotiate its frames. "Play is performative involving players, directors,
spectators, and commentators in a quadralogical exchange that, because
each kind of participant often has her or his own passionately pursued
goals, is frequently at cross-purposes" (1988, 5). The "quadralogue"
Schechner cites is from Sutton-Smith's (1979, 297) work regarding the
idea of dialogue. The term refers to four human components: the group
that stages the event as actors; the audience that receives this communication; the group that directs the proceedings; and finally, the commentators
and critics "who may not even be present at the event but whose discourse
affects not only future performances but the ways in which past events are
received" (Schechner 1988, 19).

The "slipperiness and silliness" of play makes the phenomenon almost
impossible to define, as Mechling suggests: "The study of play is about
nothing less than human nature, even if that nature is as ambiguous as play
itself" (2000, 365, 370). Clearly, I am not the first researcher to trip over
the intricate steps people perform within and between interweaving frames
of play. Huizinga, a pioneer of play studies, lamented the amount of "false
play" in today's civilization, where "it increasingly becomes difficult to tell
where play ends and non-play begins" (1950, 211). Schechner observes that
"play creates its own (permeable) boundaries and realms: multiple realities
that are slippery, porous, and full of creative lying and deceit" (1988, 5). And

Turner has judged play to be undefinable: "It is a transient and is recalcitrant to localization, to placement, to fixation—a joker in the neuroanthropological act" (1983, 233). The ambiguity of Every 15 Minutes, with its playful activities and paradoxical ideas, resounds in participants' testimonies. The world of the mundane and the world of the virtual are both in play here, and while everyone knows it isn't real, they say emphatically, "This is no joke!"

4

Engrossed Out
Every 15 Minutes as Folk Drama

Tom was snuffling, now, himself—and more in pity of himself than anybody else . . . He
was sufficiently touched by his aunt's grief to long to rush out from under the bed and
overwhelm her with joy—and the theatrical gorgeousness of the thing appealed strongly to
his nature, too, but he resisted and lay still.

—Mark Twain, *The Adventures of Tom Sawyer*

THE MOMENTUM OF EVERY 15 MINUTES, AS WELL as other related phenomena that target "impressionable youth" while sweeping entire communities
into the act, embodies a surge in contemporary folk drama. These events'
theatrical elements are apparent, and in their participants' own terms, they
are dramas (despite ubiquitous exclamations about their "reality"). Through
the staged tragedies of drunk driving, shooting sprees, sex and drugs and
suicide, participants are intended to learn the lessons of experience. As we
have seen, however, this particular kind of experience unfolds in a special
space where realism and fantasy alternate and coexist.

A phenomenon like Every 15 Minutes defies scholarly attempts to
define and explain it. Do these folk dramas produce or require collaboration and engrossment, and does their "success" hinge on such factors? This
chapter addresses these issues, describing participants' multivocal responses
to the drama, their perceptions of what makes it a success, and their enthusiasm to carry it through even when disruptions and dissent may intrude.

Every 15 Minutes programs are not simply patterned events that include
theatrical elements, such as the adolescent legend trips scholars have examined (Thigpen 1971; Ellis 1996). Like the "ostensive ordeals" documented
by both Bill Ellis and Jay Mechling among adolescents at summer camp,

DOI:10.7330/9780874218923.c04   79

THE
EL SEGUNDO POLICE DEPARTMENT
IN PARTNERSHIP WITH THE
EL SEGUNDO UNIFIED SCHOOL DISTRICT
EL SEGUNDO FIRE DEPARTMENT
ROBERT F. KENNEDY MEDICAL CENTER
COMMUNITY LEADERS AND COMMUNITY SPONSORS

EVERY
15
MINUTES

High School
May 17-18, 2001

A 2-DAY PROGRAM FOCUSING ON HIGH SCHOOL JUNIORS AND SENIORS
WHICH CHALLENGES EACH TO THINK ABOUT DRINKING, PERSONAL SAFETY
AND THE RESPONSIBILITY OF MAKING MATURE DECISIONS WHEN LIVES ARE
INVOLVED

Printed By: Kinko's, El Segundo, CA

staged crises and tragedies provide a contrived confrontation with dangerous, often supernatural, forces and a predictable, safe outcome. They are
enacted in a "spirit of pretense rather than literal belief" (Ellis 1981, 487),
and they involve an ordeal followed by a return home (reunion at the school
with classmates and families) and debriefing. However, as Ellis points out,
genuine drama differs from legend trips and related rituals; these differences
are evident in Every 15 Minutes.

In folk drama, the distinction between players and spectators is clearly
marked. (Ellis contends that even the actors in legend trips are ultimately
spectators, acting in their own real-life environments.) While the participants in Every 15 Minutes are plucked from the ranks of the student body,
and they play the (somewhat larger-than-life) roles of their actual selves,
they are prominently set apart from their peers as they march solemnly past
the bleachers under face paint and candlelight.

The self-conscious nature of E15M's enactment blurs the line between
presentation and representation, creating a hybrid of fictional narrative

and reality show. This genre of performance appears to be a growing trend. (Certainly in the realm of television, the twenty-first century has borne witness to an explosion of "scripted reality" shows in which lines of fiction and nonfiction have been obliterated.) Mock tragedies unfold in simulations staged around the country, with public schools and law-enforcement agencies rehearsing their responses to crisis. Hundreds of students and community members play the victims, while police, medical and fire crews, and members of the news media typically play themselves. As a full-fledged folk drama, E15M incorporates supernatural characters as well, represented by the uncanny cloaked figure of the Grim Reaper. Such "liminal monsters" (Mechling 1980, 48), blatantly self-conscious dramatizations, may be a way for participants to render threatening ideas (such as drug abuse and death) more manageable (Ellis 1981). Even among folk dramas, E15M is unique in its fascinating combination of ambiguous roles, as chapter 3 illustrated; some participants portray supernatural characters, while others portray *themselves* as characters in a fictional situation (i.e., as walking ghosts).

An intriguing tension hovers between the realm of the Living Dead and the rest of the school population, which looks on and comments with a range of facial expressions and body language. (The spectators' expressions themselves are often ambiguous, often self-conscious, and always open to interpretation, as I will demonstrate further.) The selection of the Living Dead tends to be a big issue for all involved, both students and adults. Sometimes most of the chosen come from the popular crowd, and the rest of the school resents them. They possess a distinguished status for this brief and exciting interlude. "It's seen as kind of a cool thing to do," said an assistant principal, "when sometimes doing the right thing and being cool do not necessarily mesh." (Playing a part in the public spectacle appeals to more students than simply participating in their school's SADD group, said one of only five SADD members active at her school. "It's not the most popular club," she remarked bitterly.) The Living Dead eagerly anticipate their reapings; one high school principal recalled, "Some kids were disappointed because they weren't taken till the end of the day." Another school's "Behavior Eligibility Policy" permitted only students with no history of emotional or alcohol problems to participate in extracurricular activities—ironically, including E15M. The Living Dead get to miss classes, go on the overnight retreat (often at a fancy hotel), eat free pizza and unlimited snacks, and transgress normal school boundaries while making their own aesthetic contribution to a creative project. They do one another's death makeup, write poetry to read at the assembly, and decorate their own graveyards. One newspaper report depicted students jumping up and down on the trunk, roof, and hood of a car to be used in the accident scene to give those parts the proper dented appearance (Reutter 2000).

In addition, as I will illustrate further in chapter 5, the Living Dead bathe in glory. They get undivided attention from special counselors; their lives are honored in the ubiquitous eulogies. Watching Every 15 Minutes take place, I am always struck by the fawning obituaries of the Living Dead—often published in the paper, posted in the cafeteria, on in-school TV monitors and even on local TV stations. (At one E15M retreat I attended, the Living Dead were preoccupied with seeing themselves on that evening's news until their counselor appeased them by promising to have her husband tape it.) A well-resourced high school near Los Angeles sent its Living Dead to a hotel where, as a "cathartic workshop," they created their own tombstones on large sheets of paper, illustrating them with flowers, hearts, and crosses. As I observed after this activity, the "deceased" enjoyed hot tubs and hijinks throughout the night, with little supervision to enforce the rules (which included, for example, "No outside phone calls" and "Don't leave the hotel"). Bleary-eyed at the assembly the next morning, they faced their tombstones posted on the far wall of the gymnasium.

All this special treatment has implications for the willing collaboration of the community as a whole, as the student body is asked to fulfill the more passive role of respectful spectators and mourn their "dead" classmates. Not everyone warms to the prescribed role. "We had students on campus that were pelting [the Living Dead] with little paper wads, because they know they can't talk back," admitted one counselor. At a Maryland retreat, some Living Dead students complained about classmates' responses: "My friends kept making jokes"; "My teacher tried to yell over the siren noise"; "Some kids yelled cuss words at me or mocked me: 'You're okay, you'll be fine!'"

The distinctions between player and spectator may be clearly defined; but are they consistently adhered to? One program's organizer described an unexpected contribution that she said enhanced the scene in her town: a passerby (who "happened to be a drama teacher") decided to contribute to the mock crash by "flying out from the audience screaming and crying and carrying on . . . She was so good that, I mean, it brought a lot more reality to it. So we're going to use her again this year, 'cause she is terrific. She hit the [local newspaper's] front page."

When friends of the Living Dead or other members of the student body audience react with high emotion that garners public attention, often soliciting concern and comfort from peers and counselors, the boundary between actor and audience is permeated. Even in the generally rigid separation at the assembly, people may cross over quite spontaneously, as when an alumnus who had been among the Living Dead two years earlier came back to see his Maryland school's E15M assembly and ended up coming onstage to speak out about the impression the program had made on him as a student. Teachers and students notice and comment with interest on who among the audience loses composure; spectators who seem particularly devastated can contribute as much intrigue to the drama as those whose "deaths" they mourn.

WILLINGNESS TO ACT "AS IF"

Bill Ellis (1981, 2001) has emphasized the importance in folk drama of participants' recognition of the fictional nature of events (as in camp mock ordeals like the "Majaska Hunt" and the "Real Snipe Hunt"). This characteristic of "genuine drama" distinguishes it from rituals such as legend trips or "pseudo-ostensive hoaxes," according to Ellis. Working from Goffman's conception of genuine drama (which, explains Ellis, "depends on all participants seeing the event in the same way"—as a fiction), (Ellis 2001, 166) this scholar demonstrates how, in the "ostensive ordeals" he studied, players create and maintain a make-believe frontier adventure, a fantasy in which campers and counselors collaborate. Without such a shared perspective, he writes, these mock ordeals could not succeed; if the counselors intended to manipulate the campers into believing the scenario, the magic would be ruined the moment a participant felt tricked or truly frightened. For Ellis, therefore, the success or failure of genuine dramas like the Scouts' mock ordeals hinges on the willingness of all involved to act *as if* they believe in a mutually contrived scenario.

Every 15 Minutes, too, relies on the premise that participants will act *as if* the tragedy is real. Those who stage it, even as they strive to "really shake up" the teenagers in attendance, are not trying to convince their audience that their friends are literally dead; yet the rhetoric of organizers implies otherwise. "Kids, this is for real! You'd better be taking this seriously!" shrilled a teacher wending her way among giggling students at one crash scene. Spectator comments would sound credulous to an observer who took them at face value. For example, two students observing the crash scene conferred:

> "Carlos got arrested, and Annie also got arrested."
> "Why did *she* get arrested? She wasn't driving."
> "She was drunk."

At one suburban Maryland high school, the announcement went out over the public address system first thing in the morning: "Today, [our school] participates in Every 15 Minutes . . . It is a somber event so please respect the seriousness of it." Teachers had been warned that the program would be going on all day; many saw it more as a disruption than anything else, according to one faculty member. In this school, E15M had been conducted twice before over the past few years, and organizers spoke with the expert tone of seasoned veterans. No one expected to be shocked—among the student body "there's a lot of anticipation," said the chief of police. "They're looking forward to being involved in it, seeing their friend dead!" he added, laughing.

But administrators generally advocate the value of surprise. Rejecting the idea of having students themselves organize the event (as some SADD chapters do), a teacher in a suburb of Washington, DC, said that would be "like having the kids wrap their own gifts. No one's going to be impressed with it if they already know all about it." The SADD advisor at a neighboring school agreed: "It will be old hat to the students if they've already seen it before." An assistant principal in Massachusetts expressed similar caution. "You have to watch out for overkill," he told a *Boston Globe* reporter in 1996. "We won't do this every year. It would lose its effect" (Nealon).

Some administrators try to keep the whole event under wraps until the day it unfolds, but they must warn the teachers of the impending classroom interruption, and in the programs I documented, invariably word had leaked out, through someone's carelessness, curiosity, or urge to gossip. Most organizers I interviewed at various schools said the identity of the Living Dead was closely guarded information, with participants sworn to secrecy until their "reaping." But conversations with students revealed that legions of siblings, friends, and teammates had the inside scoop. Word travels fast in schools, especially if the corridors are about to fill with policemen. The uncertainty of not knowing who will be reaped *next*, or exactly when it will happen, is sufficient to keep the students on edge, some organizers asserted. As a rule, however, I detected little suspense in the methodical classroom visits of the Grim Reaper. Often, I followed him along with a crowd of giggling, poking, interrogative students.

Dramas *can* fall apart and lose their participants' willingness to continue them as tradition (as Ellis demonstrates with mock ordeals) when differences in perspective turn the event into a hoax or fabrication, with those not "in the know" ending up feeling truly terrified and then deceived and betrayed. In some instances, administrators have used E15M in this way: for example, at a Los Angeles suburban high school in April 2000, administrators "tired of students responding apathetically to warnings about drugs and alcohol decided to tell them a lie—for their own good" (Garrison 2000).

They convened all the seniors at an assembly and, according to the *Los Angeles Times,* "somberly informed them that two of their classmates had been in a drunk-driving accident the night before. One was dead. The other was seriously injured." The deception was revealed at the end of the assembly, but students and parents were outraged at being so misled and traumatized. The overwhelmingly negative reaction caused officials to reconsider their plans to repeat the "skit" (as they called it) the following year (Garrison 2000).

Although few schools have pushed the Every 15 Minutes concept over the line by deceiving students in this way, such hoaxes occasionally are attempted by zealous officials (Hoffman 2008). An Iowa school in 2002 directed students to the building's foyer, where in a coffin lay an ostensibly deceased classmate who had disappeared during the program (which he had lobbied to bring to the school) the day before. Students expressed resentment when the ruse was revealed (Associated Press 2002). In 2008, a high school in Oceanside, California, caused a media stir when it sent California Highway Patrol officers into twenty classrooms to inform students their friends had been killed in alcohol-related crashes over the weekend (Carroll 2008; Hoffman 2008). This stunt, inspired by E15M's model but diverging from the standard script, caused an uproar among students but generated few parent complaints. "They were traumatized, but we wanted them to be traumatized," a guidance counselor explained to the press. Some students became hysterical, and one who spoke to the media expressed her outrage but also a sense of guilt: "You feel betrayed by your teachers and administrators, these people you trust . . . But then I felt selfish for feeling that way, because, I mean, if it saves one life it's worth it" (Hoffman 2008). The ubiquitous slogan used to justify mock tragedies was

powerful enough to temper—or at least muzzle—her anger at the adults'
emotional manipulation.

Such hoaxes have caused outrage, but apparently not enough to result
in serious consequences for the administrators who orchestrated them. On
discussion forums of online news stories, most comments condemn these
tricks as disrespectful if not dangerously traumatizing. Many who post comments make the distinction between the hoaxes and the traditional E15M
scenario, which is always openly announced and recognized as a simulation.

Why is there so little discussion among the adults involved or observing?
Why have we not seen lawsuits from parents whose children were severely
distraught by the pretense? Why do the occasional events that go awry fail to
spark a wider debate about the ethics of trauma as educational tactic? After
the Oceanside event, *San Francisco Chronicle* columnist Jon Carroll (2008)
pointed out the hypocritical aspects of the approach, including the inaccurate statistic in the title. He mockingly suggested that Oceanside's sanguine
parents might not be so accepting if the tables were turned and a policeman
falsely informed them of their child's suicide. (Of course, in E15M parents *do* "experience" the simulated loss.) Carroll aptly identifies the power
imbalance that pervades the high school system, where adults decide how
students can best be taught, engaged, and transformed. Adults' perceptions
of teenagers as thoughtless, ignorant, or apathetic frequently saturate Every
15 Minutes programs, rendering students' rights and integrity secondary
to the end goal of preventing them from drinking and driving. E15M has
never been proven to achieve that end. But for an anxious community, the
belief justifies the means.

In fact, adults and students alike are frequently willing collaborators in
the creepy pageant of Every 15 Minutes. They may be eager for the chance
to star as sinners, killers, and victims. Often their affinities for certain roles
are openly expressed. The boy who played the Grim Reaper in an Ohio
town "played it up to the max," said his high school's SADD advisor. "He
asked—his father is a minister, and he wanted and wanted to do it." As the
advisor explained, the priest who volunteered to deliver the eulogy at the
mock funeral was a last-minute replacement, but "he fit the bill perfectly
because he's a real fire-and-brimstone type, got people fired up." A parent
volunteer in Southern California spoke approvingly of a mother who was
to read her letter aloud at the assembly: "She'll do very well at this, because
she gets emotional real easily." And in that town, the Grim Reaper reveled
in his role:

The first year they did it, they asked for volunteers, and I jumped right up, saying I want to do it! . . . At Halloween I always dress up either as a vampire or, you know, some victim that looks like they've been in a terrible auto accident. I set my yard up like a cemetery scene. I have tombstones . . . In my office right now, I've got gas masks hanging on the wall, I've got pictures of cemeteries and stuff like that. I really like cemeteries! I mean, it sounds weird. But I love going into old cemeteries.

ENGROSSMENT

Ellis's work, as well as Sabina Magliocco's on haunted houses (1985), ascribes importance to the attitude Goffman termed "being engrossed." When participants are "willing collaborators in unreality," contends Ellis, they are neither completely terrified nor skeptical, but ready to suspend disbelief during the high drama of the event.

Can Ellis's model help to determine whether Every 15 Minutes, as a form of folk drama, "works"? Based on the events I have researched, I doubt that it can. But here—or anywhere—it is simply impossible to gauge true levels of engrossment. As Ellis concedes, "It is the perception of the event that defines its nature, and such a perception is no simple thing to characterize" (2001, 172). As for success, Mechling points out that even in a simple folklore event, participants may have "dramatically different motives and understandings of the event and still interact 'successfully,' that is, in a way satisfying both to the participants and to the folklorist observing the event" (1989b, 315).

The students who lingered in front of the main hallway's trophy case filled with their obituaries, gazing at their own pictures and at the sentimental tributes written by their parents, might have been reassessing their mortality and searching their souls; or they might have been enjoying a moment in the spotlight, a brilliant break from otherwise mundane high school life. Girls in the Living Dead recounted how their answering machines were full of messages from their bereaved friends, some of whom even came to the house with flowers or "tattooed" the names of the victims on their arms with Sharpie pens. Evidence like this seems to point to the engagement of participants in the drama. Those who "grieve" for the Living Dead may enjoy the public attention; one school in New Mexico set up a "wake" in the lecture hall during the day, having students from the drama department crying around a coffin to represent the family of the victim. "It was done very dramatically with lighting and stuff, and kids could come to the door and look in," a teacher said, laughing. "They were actually crying. I think they had hyped themselves up."

Are the tears a genuine or contrived display—or both? Can an observer really know the difference, and does it matter? Gary Ebersole, a historian of religion who has written on ritualized weeping and affective expression, asserts that it is not the scholar's role to judge whether tears are real or fake. Tears, whether shed privately or performatively, "must be understood in terms of the local sociocultural 'feeling rules,' moral values, aesthetics and politics," he notes; through the process of "naturalization" of tears, individuals' internalization of social rules, values, and feelings can easily lead to "seemingly spontaneous tears in specific situations" (2000, 213). Thus Ebersole warns against "the temptation to judge all tears in terms of their immediate association with 'real' emotions" (213). "Tear-filled eyes produce blurred vision," he says; "so does projecting our assumptions about tears on other peoples and times" (222).

It is difficult to know what to make of the emotional displays that occur during the course of the E15M program. As I recorded my impressions, my notes seemed to constantly diverge from the impressions stated by program organizers. Facial expressions, mutterings, gestures, and attitudes are open to endless interpretation, and this has concerned me at every school. I was aware that much was going on that I could not capture, on the surface and under it. Each person's response to the event was individual and complex. I absorbed as much as possible of what was said and done on the public stage. In interviews, though, I sometimes got hints of participants' deeper private motivations and reactions, glimpses of their past experiences of tragedy or addiction, or explanations of their political conflicts with others involved. A researcher, no matter how sensitive, has little access to the backstage emotions; tears do not necessarily relate directly to the immediate action. "The nurses end up breaking down too [along with the parents]," said a hospital worker participating in a Southern California E15M simulation, "because it just flashes back to every dead kid you've ever seen."

Such intricately layered information makes comparative analysis exceedingly difficult. How can we detect patterns of experience, when so much of what participants think and feel remains below the surface, or surfaces long after the event? The majority of adults I talked with expressed the belief that the student body was caught up in the dramatic scenario, and to my bewilderment they often described the spectators' reactions in ways that starkly contradicted my own observations. Students' facial expressions that appeared bored or skeptical to me were interpreted by E15M facilitators as "in shock" and "horrified." At an urban Southern California school, I noted the boisterous cheer that went up from the audience in the bleachers when the firefighters finally pried off the top of a car with the Jaws of Life; but later, the media arts teacher who videotaped the program for the assembly marveled at how, when they cut the roof off the car, "there was no catcalling—it all quieted down! That's the magic of *live* theater!" And the coordinator from California Alcoholic Beverage Control who had provided the dean with funding, advice, and a manual with implementation guidelines, gave a similar characterization of this crowd and of others: "All the programs are successful," he claimed. "I haven't seen a program that *wasn't* successful. I watch the students in the crowd, and most of the time about 99 percent of them are watching, the girls are in tears. That's my estimation—99 percent. There's only one or two goofballs in the crowd."

I am reluctant to assign meanings or intentions to the stares and silences of the teenagers; their attendance is mandatory, their attention is fluid, and they lead inner lives and extracurricular lives inaccessible to my outsider's eyes. But I am struck by the remarks of adult insiders like one New Mexico administrator who gushed that "90 percent of the kids at the assembly were in tears!" My own eyes had taken in a gymnasium packed with yawning, fidgeting, unfocused students.

Whatever one makes of this gap in perception, it underscores the complexity of experience in E15M. The program's undertaking involves multiple sources and levels of participation in the community; and in the planning and execution, consensus is elusive, unanimous agreement unheard of. The priorities and beliefs of diverse groups, including teachers, parents, and law-enforcement personnel, all compete and invest in this emotionally charged endeavor. If there is a collaborative vision, it is highly susceptible to breakdown.

Ubiquitous glitches, objections, and other mutterings prevent these productions from sweeping everyone up in a collective suspension of disbelief—and no matter how smoothly things may go, the multiplicity of reactions and opinions precludes the unanimous engagement that Goffman and Ellis describe in their theories. Yet in some sense, all these imperfect versions of Every 15 Minutes do seem to "work": they elicit tears and trembling in a visible minority, they reap glowing evaluations from administrators, and they continue to proliferate. Consistently, I have found consensus among players in Every 15 Minutes that the drama "hit home," that "other schools should do it too," that "we should do it every year," that "my little sister wants to be one of the accident victims cause she saw me get killed this year," and so forth.

Evidently, this drama's "success" does not require engrossment—my observations show that things never go as smoothly as planned, routinely interrupting any ideal state of engrossment. Yet organizers' assessments of E15M are overwhelmingly positive. "We had 2,300 kids out there, and you could hear a pin drop," a Texas police officer declared. Even programs that suffered serious missteps (like one in Maryland where the principal abruptly cut short the assembly before half the Living Dead had read their emotional letters to their parents, leaving the unlucky ones sobbing with rage) garnered the generic praise, "If just one life was saved, it was a success."

Many of these favorable pronouncements are made after the two-day ordeal is complete, and they contradict the complaints and disagreements expressed by the same participants during the process. Despite the *unco*operative dynamics throughout the drama, and despite the kind of "active disbelief" that interferes with the "right mood" (Ellis 2001, 173), the artifice of this production is powerful enough to leave veteran officers, educators, and a vocal contingent of students rhapsodizing over its emotional impact.

Given the ambiguity and impenetrability of much of the response to E15M—from spectators' blank faces to taunts of kids in the hallways to sarcastic comments of teachers—it is important, when examining the phenomenon, to pay attention to what and *who* keeps it going, and who puts up subtle and not-so-subtle resistance. The crucial agents and personalities are adults as well as students. As often as not, it's the adults whose personalities and conflicts complicate or derail a smooth performance.

Both adults and teenagers may compete for attention, jockey for lead roles, and covet the outpouring of affection and regret that shower down on the idealized "dead." Some parents fiercely promote their children for starring parts in the program, as one Maryland organizer recounted: "Parents were coming up wanting guarantees their kid would be among the Living Dead . . . Once they realized it would be selection, and not based on parent volunteerism, they started e-mailing and calling, kind of threatening, saying, 'I won't help out if my kid won't be in it—[it's a] waste of my time. If I come to the meeting today will you guarantee my kid will be chosen? Is the administration picking kids they like best? If that mom volunteers, will she get preference?'"

Grown-ups do not always play cooperatively with others; one program coordinator complained, "I have a lot of anger toward my department for not giving me support, guidance . . . my supervisor hasn't really done anything . . . he wasn't able to help me at all. So I've gone into this completely blind faith here."

After-the-fact accounts from organizers rarely mention the kind of outbursts and teasing that I have witnessed each time I have followed the Grim Reaper on his rounds, nor do they describe the distracted and rowdy audiences at assemblies. As Ellis (1981) has noted with campers' mock ordeals, overt skepticism can easily detract from the general mood; spectators "not taking the program seriously" dishearten those students who invest themselves in the role-play. However, I have never seen mockery or dissent result in a judgment that the program had "failed." In fact, at times, uncontrolled moments led to memorable breaks in the script, and gripping effects.

At a suburban Maryland school, the Living Dead complained bitterly about the response they got from students and teachers throughout the day. Teachers continued to talk or play videotapes while the Grim Reaper pulled students from their classrooms; kids jeered and provoked them in the hallways as they went through their day mute and white faced. Hecklers called out to the cloaked figure:

> "He's not even that Grim!"
> "He's a monk!"
> "He's Darth Vader!"
> "*Yeah,* Grim Reaper!" [*fist pumping*]
> "I am Satan!" [*deep voice*]
> "Nice shoes!"
> "*I* wanted to die!"

The crash victim role-players reported that some kids threw rocks at the cars set up for the accident scene. Rules were discarded right and left. After months of preparation and anticipation, one Living Dead boy skipped school on the big day. A Living Dead girl had to leave at midday to testify in court against a teacher who was being sued for sexual misconduct. A parent waited at home all day for a death notification that never came. The principal had decreed (somewhat arbitrarily, to avoid overcrowding) that only students in "B Lunch" could go outside to see the mock accident; but when the designated hour arrived, students poured out of the building with or without permission from their teachers. They viewed the proceedings and offered commentary:

> "This is kind of gay."
> "This is retarded."
> "I'm going to be quoted in the *Washington Post!*"
> "*I* want to go to jail! Take *me* to jail!"
> "It's better than sitting in philosophy [class]."
> "Is that girl [in the audience] really crying? Come on! These
>   people are alive!"
> "This sucks—last year's accident was better."

The police department's E15M coordinator was particularly disturbed to find out at the last minute that two of the Living Dead had received special permission to come back to life for an important baseball game that afternoon, thanks to their coach's political influence over the principal. Furthermore, the coach himself had been slated to join the ranks of the "reaped" to signify to the teenagers that drunk driving could cost them their mentors as well as their peers. In a disgusted tone, the police coordinator told me: "One of the things that I'm not really happy with is that two male students, one is the drunk driver and the other is a Living Dead person, are playing in a baseball game after school today. I'm very against it. Along with the teacher who is being pulled, he's one of the teachers being pulled! He is a well-known, well-liked teacher, who happens to be the coach of the baseball team. So right after all this, rather than them going to the funeral home, they're going to play baseball."

Yet at this school, in spite of all the discontent and subversion, a powerful moment occurred during the assembly the next morning. The Living Dead had rehearsed their speeches before the assembly began, and the presentations moved fluidly from one speaker to the next until the girl who had played one of the crash victims suddenly stopped and addressed a group of students at the back of the lecture hall: "It's people like you that are laughing that make this so hard for the rest of us. And I don't know who threw rocks at the cars yesterday, but it was really immature!" She then went back to her speech. This unexpected interlude, confronting the negative, disrespectful behavior that had been part of the event since the first appearance of the Grim Reaper in the locker hall, constituted a dramatic break in the program. The lecture hall, containing more than 600 teenagers, became quiet immediately, and no more laughing was audible for the rest of the assembly.

Whether or not they are consciously striving for an experience of engrossment, participants are bound to drift in and out of it as events unfold. "The show must go on," shrugged an administrator in Los Angeles when one of her Living Dead left temporarily to attend a school open house with her parents (supposedly isolated from her for the duration of E15M). At another school, when the student who was "killed" in the mock crash choked up during his speech, his mother ran onto the stage to join him, pulling out tissues to wipe his face and staying there, sobbing into his shoulder, until he had finished. And in a small industrial city in Ohio, a program organizer related the ups and downs of his school's event:

> The president of MADD was so boring! She demanded we show slides, and they weren't in order . . . I told her to keep it short and sweet, get to the point, but she dragged it on and it lost interest. But our memorial service was tremendous—we had a priest giving a eulogy, and we used all the tear-jerking music we could find. We originally had a gospel choir ready to go but they got pulled out at the last minute because of a discipline problem. But instead there was a duet with two seniors from the choir. It gave me goose bumps, seriously.

"We were definitely guided with that decision," chimed in his female colleague. "Divine intervention came in and saved our ass!"

"This is kind of like planning a wedding. The day gets here, and you're like, 'Well, here we go, it's either going to run smoothly, or we'll be adaptable!'" one Southern California policeman told me jovially as we drove to a school about to begin its third Every 15 Minutes in six years. Here, in one of the communities that first developed the program, an attitude of confident expertise pervaded the huge corps of parent volunteers. Police and administrators joked easily with each other, and adults and students alike told me repeatedly what a tight-knit community this was, how "everybody knows everybody." The school was being renovated, which threw a slight wrench into the Grim Reaper's rounds, since classroom schedules had been switched around unexpectedly. The tall, cloaked specter dismissed the problem:

> There are little glitches—like the girl's not in the classroom where she's supposed to be so you have to run—she was supposed to be in the first room I went to, and when I called her name and nobody got up, I thought, "What happened here, are we in the wrong room?" It was the second room I went into this period. When I called her name nobody got up—her schedule's been changed or something. It turned out she was in *this* classroom, so somebody

had to run down to the attendance office and find out what class—little
bumps like that. But nothing major at all.

Although teachers at this school tended to continue their class activities
when the Grim Reaper entered, this was *not* interpreted negatively as it had
been at the Maryland schools I observed. Amid a general atmosphere of
informed and willing collaboration, these teachers' choice was well received
by participants. The Grim Reaper explained: "The teacher just let the video
run, and I think that's more impactful, because you never know when death
is going to call you, and life doesn't stop just before that happens, or just
before you're killed, or death comes and knocks at your door . . . all of a
sudden you could just be called, and your time is up. Like I said before, the
world doesn't stop before you die, and I think by continuing teaching or
letting the video go, I think that sends that message."

The easy collaboration and thorough planning of organizers here did
not leave them immune to unanticipated complications: a student fainted
during gym class immediately before the mock accident was scheduled to
begin, creating a real-life emergency, and the subsequent juggling of ambulances and personnel caused minor chaos and major delays. However, the
enthusiasm of the town—local folks had brought beach chairs to set up in
front of the school, for a good view of the accident scene—seemed to carry
the program through any and all missteps. "This is like the Fourth of July
for us!" exclaimed one spectator. "Everybody comes out for it—we're a very
supportive town." Exceptions included a hysterical phone call from a local
mother who passed the accident scene on her way home from the grocery
store. ("She was freaking out: 'Why didn't you tell us?' God, it's only been
advertised all over the place!" said a police officer's wife, disgusted.) Despite
all the confusing distractions and renovations, organizers proclaimed the
event a great success in the end.

Likewise, E15M survived unexpected complications during the course
of its performance at a school in California; a downpour of rain on the day
of the program made all kinds of things go wrong, but that only added to
the desperate and miserable feeling of the day, which made all the more
impact, according to a student who attended the event. A hospital morgue
tour for the Living Dead in Maryland was canceled at the last minute due
to a financial scandal; hospital administrators "didn't want kids running
around in the morgue when they were being investigated." Observing Every
15 Minutes in a small city east of Los Angeles, I saw paramedics accidentally

load the wrong girl into the helicopter, which then had to return to the school to exchange crash victims. The film crew, trying to keep up with all the action, was in a state of confusion; but organizers remained enthusiastic about the program's overall impact.

In communities less unified, miscommunications may have more serious implications for engrossment in E15M's drama, as in an urban Los Angeles area school with predominantly minority students, where the dean in charge of the program pulled it off in the face of bitter opposition from some groups of parents. Two supportive parents, volunteering in the makeup room, explained:

> There was some opposition to it, I think because this is a very large Asian community and a lot of the parents are Asian immigrants, and death is a tricky subject . . . in Asian cultures, we do not talk about death! It's not something you talk about at all!

> They were a little upset because this program is actually optional, if as a parent you don't want your child to observe it, or be in it, they can opt out. They sent out "negative permission slips"—but, unfortunately, there wasn't enough time to get it translated, so it didn't go out in all the like fifteen languages that are spoken here!

Parental objections arise commonly. "We need to have kids with more socioeconomic and ethnic diversity," acknowledged a Maryland police coordinator, "but for Asians, it's a huge culture no-no!" Personal as well as cultural attitudes influence participation. "My mom wouldn't write my obit—said it's playing with death," complained a Maryland girl who was cut from the Living Dead and relegated to makeup duty after her parents backed out. In a Los Angeles suburb, one mother described how she changed her mind about taking part: "We have our own cable TV station here, and the cable expresses everything, in fact this program will be shown on cable, for everyone who wants to watch it. And that's how it captivated me. The reason for that was really funny—I did *not* want to get involved the first time around, because I thought, Ugh! [*shudder*] That sounds too weird! Right? But when I watched it on television is when I realized the impact, all the effort that goes into putting this one message across."

As chapter 5 will further explore, the appeal of the public and media attention motivates many participants to get past their hesitations about the mock scenario's creepy aspects. But not everyone can be convinced; as the determined Los Angeles dean admitted in an interview before her program, the teachers were "going to be pissed" at the interruption to their classes, added to the frequent intrusions of state testing on their lesson time. Some oppose the tactics of E15M for philosophical reasons, as well, like teachers who "felt that the students were pretty sheltered at this high school and that it would be bad for them to be exposed to something so traumatic," explained a parent. Just as commonly, though, the perception that kids are sheltered or "think they are invincible" is cited as the precise reason they could benefit from a wake-up call delivered through the shocking simulation of disaster.

A DRAMA WITH A HUMAN HEARTBEAT

The line that traces a patient's heartbeat on an EKG machine is known as a "tracing." It shows disturbances in the normal rhythm of the heartbeat; yet not every flutter or abnormality signifies a fatal heart attack. If one were to draw a tracing for each version of E15M, I suspect that each program would show at least one significant disturbance along the line. In fact, it would be impossible to find a version of Every 15 Minutes that does not include deviations from the "ideal" rhythm. Yet the drama and its players continue, adapting and responding to these moments of crisis, and receiving applause at the end.

So what keeps the play alive, instead of its dying from the inevitable murmurs, palpitations, and attacks? The human factor plays a crucial part: how readily participants react to spontaneity and change, how they deal with disagreements in organizational structures, or how skilled they are at resuscitation techniques. "Homemade cookies are really the key," suggested the parent in charge of food at one event. "It's extremely important to have homemade cookies to make the kids feel supported." Perhaps success also depends on elusive, mystical factors involving faith and spirituality. But success does not depend on constant and complete engrossment in the drama, nor loyalty to the prescribed script.

Each event I have documented, whether through firsthand observation or interviews alone, has been judged worthwhile by those in charge, and they have kept it alive by repeating it and passing it on to other schools, establishing it as tradition. Something stable and powerful enough in the premise, the structure, and the images of this drama appeals broadly and consistently to people in a vast range of local contexts.

Death itself is inevitable yet shocking—and participants frequently emphasize this paradox. "Even though you know everything that is going to happen, it's still so shocking when you actually go through it," say the Living Dead and the parents who receive death notifications from police officers while their kids are being "reaped" at the school. "People, this *can and will* happen to you," one counselor gravely told his students. Another program coordinator explained to me, "These kids know they're going to die, but they don't know when—that's part of the 'reality' too."

Like death, and like the mock accidents in E15M, folk drama as a form is both scripted and ever changing. E15M, as a recognizable performance, exhibits remarkable stability—and yet it naturally evolves in response to local and generational tastes. "The first year, we had a judge talk [at the assembly], but nobody liked it so we got rid of him," said a Maryland county police chief. Although his Living Dead inspected coffins at the local funeral home, the chief nixed the idea of a morgue tour as "a little too dramatic— we'd have parental and teacher concerns." A Texas sergeant described the delicate decisions involved in assembly planning: "We have talked about in the future putting a coffin out front of the auditorium with a mirror in it, or having it onstage and then at the assembly have two students, male and female, come out in prom attire, but with injuries and makeup, and just stand there by the coffin. We're constantly trying to put a little different twist on it and do what we can to make it as effective as possible. With these kids you can't have anything hokey, it's got to get their attention."

We have seen that each E15M event emerges within its situational context and with its inescapable human element. As shown in chapter 3, it is impossible to mark out distinctly the points at which humans step across from role-play into the realm of authentic empathy and emotional response. These shifts cannot be controlled or even documented reliably. But often, unplanned moments only add to the life of the drama—breaking the frame within which E15M's accidents are staged, they can produce a "gasp" that brings people into, or at least closer toward, a state of engagement.

My research has shown that even with a program as full of extreme imagery as Every 15 Minutes, administrators tout a paradigm of sticking to the script, following the rules, and "staying true to the program." However, in the situated enactment of the scenario, the Grim Reaper is a real person, not a polished professional actor. He is a policeman whose hobby is visiting graveyards, or a local football player who flirts with the girls in the hall, or a clumsy giant from the senior class who removes his hood under the hot sun at the crash scene, gives the Living Dead backrubs, and jabs their rear ends with his scythe. Students molest him in the hallways; he wanders into the wrong classroom looking for his next victim; his cloak gets caught in the door of the departing hearse.

I have witnessed these and many other cracks disturbing the scenario's smooth progression. When a student sarcastically cried out, "Oh, boo hoo hoo!" during the policeman's reading of an obituary, he was sent to the principal's office and suspended. A teacher brought his two noisy toddlers to psychology class on E15M day, and they babbled through the obituary; the mother of the "crash victim" complained that the *real* DUI widow who spoke of her experiences was "too long-winded, dragged on and on—she was losing the kids in the back row." A principal trying to hammer home the grim statistic at the assembly repeatedly said "every fifteen seconds" instead of "every fifteen minutes." An officer reading obituaries in classrooms stumbled over the phrase "sitting shiva" and queried, "What does that mean?" Hecklers booed the cop handcuffing the "drunk driver" ("She is very popular," noted a teacher) and urged her, "Run!" Cell phones ring during funeral home tours; kids poke the Grim Reaper and beg to be taken.

The glitches, the unplanned dramas, and the spontaneous responses of those who watch and play at E15M reveal the constant human heartbeat in the life of the folk drama. As I have noted, adjustments and missed cues are typical; some performers freeze in the spotlight, while others expand in it, or try to hog it. Still, no matter what is lost in the planned form of the drama, time and again the players find ways of adapting and concluding with satisfaction that all the cost and trouble were worth it. Remarked a California school counselor: "Nothing that glitched or got stuck was consequential to the students' experience. We just fix it, and that's just what you do, you know, the show goes on kind of idea. Somebody misses a line? You just move on to the next line, and you don't want the audience to know that you missed a line."

Why might people who were perfectly aware that this was a fictional drama work themselves into such tearful states? What might motivate them to invest such time, money, and emotional resources in establishing and continuing the tradition? Throughout my field notes and interview transcripts, those involved in the proceedings provide hints. They often talked explicitly about the "dramatic" elements of the event, mentioning the makeup, the special effects, and the fun they were having. (Some admitted their enjoyment readily, others more sheepishly.)

I am convinced that E15M participants, while weeping over their staged tragedy, may really be having the time of their lives, though they are perhaps loath to acknowledge it. Folk drama does not simply provide an expressive outlet for community anxieties; it is not simply a means of instilling values and changing teens' attitudes. For kids and adults alike, this is *fun*—the dressing up, the graphic makeup, the sirens and excitement and tears and emotional music. In the staging of mock tragedies, fun is not explicitly planned or officially sanctioned. But it is there, in the suspension of everyday routine, and in the creation of a dramatic event into which people can throw themselves without any requirement of literal belief. (Even mocking or resisting the proceedings may be far more appealing than a classroom lecture.) Participants can celebrate their own lives and deaths and then go back to normal when the bell rings.

The power of such grisly folk drama is evident as it spreads throughout America in the shape of haunted houses, emergency drills, and simulated highway tragedies in school parking lots. Lunch after death is becoming standard fare in American teenagers' cultural curriculum.

5

The Dazzle and Darkness of Play

They felt like heroes in an instant. Here was a gorgeous triumph; they were missed; they were mourned; hearts were breaking on their account; tears were being shed; accusing memories of unkindnesses to these poor lost lads were rising up, and unavailing regrets and remorse were being indulged: and best of all, the departed were the talk of the whole town, and the envy of all the boys, as far as this dazzling notoriety was concerned. This was fine. It was worth while to be a pirate, after all.

—Mark Twain, *The Adventures of Tom Sawyer*

M Y RESEARCH HIGHLIGHTS PARTICIPANTS' ATTRACTION TO THE FUN and creative elements of Every 15 Minutes, and their desire for the community attention—the "dazzling notoriety," in Twain's words—that they receive as players in the drama. The program's promoters advance the premise that its entertaining aspects make it an effective means of combating drunk driving, grabbing the kids by the nape of the neck and shaking them. Yet my data suggest that the appeal of the program lies as much in getting attention *through it* as in paying attention *to it*, as people are drawn to the chance to play an active, starring part in the event.

Play has long been idealized in academic literature. Back in 1950 Johan Huizinga argued that it is the play element in culture that has driven all of human history, and while scholars' romanticizing of play has drawn well-founded criticism from more recent theorists, including Sutton-Smith (1997), I see value in Huizinga's fundamental insight. I recommend, however, including the idea of dark play as a key element in this driving force.

Is there something weird about how much people enjoy playing at morbid topics as they do in E15M? Is such play cathartic, as many counselors and theorists suggest? Might there be a destructive quality of play? As I have

DOI:10.7330/9780874218923.c05   100

noted throughout this book, people's motives and responses are deeply layered and individual; yet a palpable undercurrent of attention seeking courses through my findings. In the following passages I illustrate the entertainment appeal of E15M, the ways in which public memorializations glorify the lives of its young stars, and the usefulness of "dark play" as a concept to understand this complex and spreading phenomenon.

EVERY 15 MINUTES AS ATTENTION GRABBER

Recruiting volunteers and raising awareness for the approaching Every 15 Minutes program in his small Southern California community, said a police coordinator, was easy. "People know it's a vital program, the kids love it, the community loves it. They do what they can. It's [publicized by] word of mouth, because we don't want to make it, you know, a *circus.*" Yet in many respects, the program uses its theatrical elements without shame to draw the public into the spectacle. "The Living Dead images, in my opinion, are sort of the eye candy," one teacher explained. "To get a message across to any person, you have to get their attention. And by getting their attention in this manner, and then the crash scene, it brings it home. That's the basis of theater."

A reporter for the *Today Show* on NBC in April 2001 compared the Living Dead faces to "makeup jobs that look like they're straight out of a horror movie." Participants' comments I heard from coast to coast reflect broad recognition of the show-business aspects of the event. "This is like a Hollywood production! It's great," exclaimed a Maryland parent hours after receiving her "death notification" from police. "My knees went weak," she recalled. Other participants, such as a Living Dead student in California, critiqued the program as though reviewing a movie: "Like, this year, I heard that the crash out front wasn't as graphic as other years were, and they didn't use really as good special effects. It wasn't as, I guess, poignant as it was before. But it still hit home really hard." At the hospital, a nurse remarked: "They're going to get a lot of good footage of the mom; I heard she's already hysterical."

The conscious effort to make the event theatrical influences myriad decisions by planners, from sticking with the "Every 15 Minutes" title ("I don't think anybody's really interested in the [statistic's] accuracy, they're interested in the emotional grab of that being a cool name for the program," said a paramedic in New Mexico) to editing the video for the assembly. "I decided to pull a trick out of Fellini's hat," one school's video tech specialist told me with enthusiasm prior to the assembly. "I went back and forth in time to give it more dramatic effect. I hope it works—the proof of the pudding is in the tasting!" I asked him how he would know if his video was affecting people in the audience. "Well, hopefully they'll cry," he answered. "My gut feeling is that people will be very moved."

Many commentators argue that a media-saturated American culture has become inured to images of violence, and E15M participants have echoed this concern; one Internet Guestbook posting read, "With reality TV warping the minds of America's youth, it is sad that a school has to kill thirty people to make a statement. However, it is a statement that needs to be made. By participating in this program or simply by observing its content, students are forever changed . . . This program is sick and disgusting, but it works." Still, the staging of E15M's grisly scenes in the educational context has caused some cringes, and communities have modified local versions to make the trauma more palatable or acceptable. An official from the California Department of Alcoholic Beverage Control told me of an unusual creative variation: "At one school they dressed the coroner up like Abe Lincoln. They made the coroner look like a nineteenth-century coroner, what somebody would think of a nineteenth-century coroner. Because they didn't want the Grim Reaper. Sometimes I think the educators are too overly concerned about their darling students, and their emotional impact—and yet their kids can watch videos and movie murders and stuff like that, and that doesn't bother them! They're worried about the Grim Reaper representing Death, that it might affect Junior!"

Yet parents I interviewed who watched the mock accident with their young children did not object to the graphic subject matter of the display; one mother observed, "If [townspeople] are just strolling along, walking with their kids, and they see it, they stop. It's like when we watch a movie. I let my kindergartner and first-grader watch *The Patriot*. Because it's about our history. And that was very graphic. And their favorite part was when that guy's head got blown off by the cannonball." Another mother offered this perspective: "I like being involved in my children's lives at school, so I am a 'room mom' in my kindergartener's class, and we went on a field trip to the insect museum—it was *disgusting!*—last week, so I was telling some of the moms about Every 15 Minutes, and they're going to come and watch this afternoon!" Evidently she found the prospect of bloody teenage "victims" less disgusting than impaled insects.

SEEKING, GETTING, AND BASKING IN ATTENTION

"Play is always multivoiced, and it intentionally conceals and reveals its meanings," writes Anna Beresin, in an essay using Batesonian frame analysis to examine the ways children have translated the images of September 11, 2001, into their games and pretend play (2002, 332). While folklorists have long studied the adaptation of cultural material (including its violent elements) into folklore expressions and children's play activities, they have tended to romanticize this process and its functions, ignoring potentially concealed meanings and agendas. Robert Lavenda (1988, 1991) has raised some of these issues in his studies of small-town beauty pageants and their multiple purposes; he demonstrates their covert competitive aspect, their backbiting and outrage, and the disputes over morality and over who deserves to win. These pageants, asserts Lavenda, matter to the way communities think about themselves and the image they want to present; "Though couched in terms of play, they are deadly serious" (1988, 168).

Brian Sutton-Smith has referred to the "hidden transcripts" of play (1997), and this serves as a valuable metaphor for contemplating the many ulterior motives of the Living Dead—including finding out what people might say about them if they weren't around, making their friends jealous, and simply getting out of school for a field trip and a night of hijinks at a hotel.

Though desire for power rarely is acknowledged explicitly by program participants, this strikes me as one important hidden transcript underlying the tearful drama of E15M. "The shedding of ritual tears can be used to 'buy' social status and prestige," notes Gary Ebersole (2000, 245). Prestige and competition have relevance here, from the selection of the Living Dead to the aesthetic appraisal of their image. During a funeral home tour, after inspecting an array of caskets, one Living Dead girl enviously admired another's ghoulish makeup: "You have the best face!"

Sutton-Smith speculates on the appeal of a sense of empowerment through play; he cites "the experience of being possessed by something other and greater than the self . . . going beyond the restrictions of everyday life." According to Sutton-Smith, through play activities "participants may surpass themselves and gain a new sense of empowerment . . . the sense that the limitations of life can be transcended" (1997, 86). Students involved in E15M who appear to be wracked by grief instantly attract the concern and caring of their peers and adult guardians. Under everyday circumstances, these students have little power to command such highly charged attention from their communities; so attending their own funerals affords an intoxicating opportunity. Within the play frame, those who are normally disempowered get to try on an experience of power and freedom along with their temporarily dead identity.

At times, I encountered counselors or parents who expressed awareness and understanding of such unstated motivations. Adults don't listen to kids enough, a parent volunteer in Maryland admitted, and kids need that outlet: "If you give them the opportunity to talk, it's like turning on a faucet that doesn't want to turn off. They want that vehicle."

Like Tom Sawyer and his pirates, participants in E15M crave the attention lavished on them by their "survivors." People are irresistibly drawn to eavesdropping on conversations about themselves, and this program provides that pleasure and pain, albeit in a virtual scenario. (The impulse is illustrated by the red-on-black lettering on one school's Living Dead T-shirts: "Would You Remember Me? RHS May 1, 2001.") A student at the retreat reflected, "Today it was interesting to see who were your true friends, who would be affected if you were gone . . . You found out what people really think about you, what they would say about you if you were gone." A student who played dead in the mock accident said later, "I wish I had seen people's faces, 'cause the way I was facing [lying in the wrecked car], I could only see the sky." And the following exchange (in friendly, possibly teasing tones) between a teacher and Living Dead student (whose name I have changed) in a small California community exemplified this self-conscious curiosity:

> Teacher [speaking to me]: They took Kari away, and then the policemen came in and talked and gave the eulogy for Kari and told us about drunk driving, and once Kari left we were talking about how much we missed her, and that we were going to be sad, because her picture was great! One of the best pictures I've seen of Kari, and it made me really miss her.
>
> Kari: Did anybody get sad?
>
> Teacher: Yeah! Totally!
>
> Kari: [When I came back to class] I was worrying that nobody cared about the fact that I was dead!
>
> Teacher: We were ignoring you! That's what we're supposed to do!

Often, the "hidden transcripts" are not so hidden after all, as people recognize the mock tragedy as a chance to perform; the spotlight may appeal to participants, amuse them, or intimidate them. "Do I get to reveal myself [to the audience] before we go?" a cloaked student playing the Grim Reaper begged his program director as she rounded up the Living Dead to leave the football field crash scene for their courthouse tour. One California town arranged for a passing motorist to call 911 and report the crash as part of the staged drama; "Okay, this is her five minutes of fame here!" commented a chuckling police officer. In contrast, the mother of one of the Living Dead told me her husband hadn't wanted to be involved because "he hates being in the limelight." Whether the fleeting chance for fame and glory is welcomed or shunned, it is undeniably a factor in E15M, often significantly contributing to the program's appeal.

The pleasures and functions of "pretend dying" have been explored by Jay Mechling (2008) in his article "Gun Play," in which he refers to the "Tom Sawyer effect" of "observing" one's own death. The playfulness (around gruesome subject material) of Every 15 Minutes is similar to genres of war play that have been explored by Mechling, yet with a unique twist of mock agony. Indeed, the romanticization of death that Every 15 Minutes exemplifies is a popular folk idea that historically has found expression in genres from literature of World War I (well documented in Paul Fussell's *The Great War in Modern Memory*) through James Dean and the conventional wisdom that "only the good die young." (The quote "Live fast, die young, and leave a good-looking corpse" is often attributed to James Dean, but was actually spoken by the actor John Derek in the 1949 film *Knock on Any Door.*)

PUBLIC MEMORIALIZATION OF THE LIVING DEAD

"More of the kids wanted to be in the wreck scene," one vice principal told me. He mused, "I don't know if it's a glamorous situation. I think they wanted to be part of something that would be everlasting in people's minds." Public commemorations of the Living Dead evoke affection, admiration, and grief (although, as an E15M website conceded, "it was just imagined grief").

During a California assembly, epitaphs designed by the Living Dead for themselves, drawn with magic marker on poster board, were displayed on the gymnasium wall—juxtaposed with the gym's "Home of the Eagles" theme, eagle mascots, murals of basketball players, championship banners, and the school song painted above the backboard. Passages from the cardboard tombstones included the following examples (in which students' names have been changed):

He loved his family and friends. He was a hard worker but he knew how to get down. He made us happy and he made us sad, but he always made us laugh.

Loving daughter, sister, granddaughter, and friend. Her sense of humor and competitive attitude will be missed greatly.

Tamara, known to everyone as Tammy, will be dearly missed by her parents, sister and family. Tammy was a very peppy girl who loved to cheerlead and hang out with friends. The beach will never be the same without that little roller skater! Tammy was never able to live her dream, to live in Hermosa Beach on the strand. She is missed by many. We all love you Tammy.

"May you live forever and may I never die," was his favorite saying. He lived every day as it came and his death was abrupt and tragic.

Stylized obituaries are posted prominently in school classrooms and hallways, in school and community newspapers, and on websites. Their tone ranges from formal to colloquial, usually falling somewhere between the two, with quirky personal details followed by hypothetical information about funeral arrangements and names of the bereaved. These lists of "survivors" often appear to include every living member of the extended family, broadening the spotlight to shine on as many people as possible. "It shows just how many people are affected by drunk driving," said one advocate; "My cousin was pissed I didn't put her in my obituary," a Living Dead student mentioned to a friend as they compared each other's memorial photos.

The excerpts below are from obituaries (posted, printed, and distributed to the public in Xeroxed packets) written by a combination of parents, students, and student government representatives who helped plan E15M at their Maryland school:

> Snowboarding was Jeff's primary avocation. He had snowboarded throughout the West and had made numerous trips to Europe. He had planned to attend the University of Colorado and vowed one day to become a professional snowboarder. Jeff had won every competition he ever entered and his prospects were excellent.

> Scott relished his acting roles in school productions including "Hello Dolly" and "Stage Door." Scott was known for his iconoclastic style. He'd wear Hawaiian shirts on cold, snowy days and sports coats and dress shirts on regular days. And who can forget his trusty Irish cap? Scott's friends and family will forever miss his outrageous sense of humor, beautiful eyes, warm smile, and caring heart.

> Kerri leaves behind a stellar list of accomplishments in the fields of academics, sports and music, but she will best be remembered by those who knew her for her uncommonly kind heart, her loyal friendship, her honest nature, and her wonderful sense of humor and fun.

> His peers, especially the "posse" will remember Matthew as a warm, fun loving and a good friend.

The Internet increasingly serves as a medium for the expression of public tributes to the "dead" students. Internet message boards like the Every15Minutes.com Guestbook, though dominated by descriptions of and praise for the program, serve also as a forum for public outpourings of love and nostalgia; and these memorializations appear for friends in both the Living Dead and the literally dead. For example, a mock accident victim was remembered by a girl who wrote, "Tara was a nice person and a good student. The thing I really liked about Tara was her personality. She was humorous, sweet, and nice. Tara was a great friend. I will miss her."

Many Guestbook visitors post tributes to friends and family who were actually killed by drunk drivers, and they direct viewers to personal websites created in honor of those lost loved ones. "I would like for you to visit my daughter's memorial website . . . she was killed a by drunk driver June 8," wrote one mother in October 2002, indicating her Web address. And a school website included a Memorial Page that combined the real and the virtual: links to memorials to members of the community who had died in alcohol-related crashes shared the screen with links to E15M victim obituaries. A list of "death links" completed the page. (These links led to poetry about death, online support groups, jokes about death and dying, discount airfares in case of death of a loved one, life insurance quotes and coverage information, and the commercial website of a wholesale distributor selling "Eternal Memories handcrafted wood caskets and urns.")

Additional features common to Every 15 Minutes programs include graveyards outside the school, flags flying at half-staff, and shrines piled with flowers, candles, and teddy bears. Those "left behind" mourn and celebrate the lives of the Grim Reaper's victims through individually creative gestures both personal and public: sentimental letters written to friends who are away at the retreat, or Living Dead names "tattooed" on their skin with felt-tip pens.

The videos depicting the entire scenario from beginning to end also romanticize and memorialize the Living Dead, and their screening at the public assembly is typically cited as one of the most powerful moments of the program. These videos usually incorporate clips of the students laughing with friends, scoring goals, playing music, and so forth, to a soundtrack of upbeat songs. Once the accident scene shatters the mood, editing choices favor slow-motion footage of participants, spectators, and families, with despairing expressions accentuated by tear-jerking music. (As noted in chapter 3, Sarah McLachlan songs and Samuel Barber's "Adagio for Strings" dominate soundtrack selections.)

One might wonder if all this public attention and memorialization does not frame death in an exaggeratedly romantic light, possibly appealing to teenagers' sensibilities to such an extent that it fosters destructive impulses. Every 15 Minutes does not explicitly or officially link death with fun and glory. One Maryland parent, however, made an unusual and telling comment in her assembly speech. "Many of you want to be on the *back page* of the yearbook with your own page, 'In Memoriam'—you don't want to blend in with the other students in the yearbook! But many people [in car accidents] *don't* die . . . Do you want to live with brain damage or some physical incapacity for years and years?" This parent, by departing from the standard E15M rhetoric and raising the threat that drunk driving might lead to *not dying*, acknowledged teenagers' need to stand out "on their own page," to be celebrated by the community, and to be everlasting in people's minds.

DARK PLAY

A student covered with fake abrasions appeared slightly sheepish about his eagerness to play his role in E15M: "I wanted to be in the crash because I have a sick mind." As a way of getting attention and having fun, simulating gruesome death and extreme grief leans toward the morbid. What draws people to such dark activities? Roger Abrahams, discussing the "paradoxical conditions of play," suggests that the appeal may lie in the opportunity to safely explore other ways of acting, free from the constraints of social customs and critiques. "Invoking license 'in play' often leads to the extension of that license to depict and explore motives that we are not permitted to examine through enactment outside that specially distanced, stylized, and intensified environment of the play-stage," writes Abrahams. "Such motives enter into the proceedings to intensify the occasion, thus making it more fun. Such inversive motives, now exempted from full judgment on moral grounds, become the embodiment of the dark side of a culture's vocabulary" (1986, 30).

Abrahams's essay describes a real wake, not a fake one, but it raises the idea that death can be connected to laughter: "Play engages with the largest movements of life, serving not only as a way of testing social and cultural boundaries in the pursuit of personal and social development, but maintaining the sense of open passage between the worlds of the dead and the living. To do this, the world of the living is rearranged and revalued, at least for the moment of the wake. Here, then, life-and-death matters are subjected to investigation in play, play in the very face of death, but in a world of laughter" (1986, 43–44).

The worlds of real death and pretend play, as Abrahams observes (and as I discuss throughout this book) can easily share space, shift their boundaries, and draw on each other for material. Although Sutton-Smith has asserted that in Western culture, children are allowed less freedom for "dark or deep play" than adults, "who are thought not to play at all" (1997, 151), Every 15 Minutes presents evidence to the contrary. By special arrangement, for the duration of the mock tragedy, people young and old have license to play with dark cultural material.

Richard Schechner refers to dark play as a process by which "alternative, even mutually contradictory, realities are brought into contact with each other," creating events that have "an atmosphere of safety and trust but, once under way, are places where very risky business can be explored" (1988, 3, 5). He notes that such play constantly erupts and transforms from serious discussion to horseplay and back again. Such examples show up everywhere in the contradiction-ridden frame of Every 15 Minutes. I agree with Schechner's opinion that "the classic distinction fencing child play off from adult play is improper," as well as that "play need be neither voluntary nor fun" (3). Sutton-Smith, too, brings insight to the phenomenon of dark play, writing that it "engenders variable contingencies (uncertainties and risks) for the purpose of exercising selective control over them in fictive or factual terms" (1997, 229). Taking up the topic of death by drunk driving, players and whole communities may exercise through E15M a measure of control over their anxieties—by deliberately managing the "experience" of death and coming back to life, by shaping their own funerals, and by embellishing their own eulogies and epitaphs.

Yet the concept of dark play has not been clearly and consistently defined in academic literature, and scholars attempting to elucidate its meaning have advanced a number of additional theories. Schechner has posited that in dark play "even the rules of play are subverted or sabotaged" (1988, 3) and that "dark play's inversions are not declared or resolved; its end is not integration but disruption, deceit, excess, and gratification" (13). He considers dark play a phenomenon in which "the play frame is absent, broken, porous, or twisted" (16). In fact, he cites drunk driving as an example of dark play where losing could mean dying.

According to this conception, in dark play some participants take the events more seriously than others; play that is experienced as dark by one person may be innocuous to someone else. Some participants may not realize what is going on is pretend and not real, writes Schechner; "Innocents, dupes, butts, [and] anxious loved ones" may be "nonplayers" whose reaction "is a big part of what gives dark play its kick" (1988, 13).

Scholars who study events of play, ritual, and theater have looked at interacting frames and interrelationships among aesthetics, play, and power (Rasmussen 1997), and Lindquist (2001) ties these connections even more tightly in her anthropological discussion of dark play. For her, the term implies power manipulations where one participant's suffering is another's fun (as in hazing, children's ganging up on each other, or even sadomasochism). As frames become "braided," she writes, they are fraught with power dynamics that seep in through the cracks. In instances where torturers play with their victims, Lindquist sees an experience of "flow" that she identifies as different from the "romantic rosiness" of most descriptions of play.

The hoaxes or fabrications that administrators have occasionally tried to pull off by matter-of-factly presenting crushed cars or death announcements to students (rather than the full-fledged drama of E15M's two-day ordeal) may resemble dark play as Schechner and Lindquist define it, using examples of brutal play, having fun at others' expense, deceit, and torture. But I argue that E15M, in its elaborated form, is simultaneously "romantic and rosy" and dark. This program combines elements of dark play (feeding on morbid and risky subject matter) with folk drama and its collaborative "willingness to act as if" the scenario were real. Neither the *real* action of driving drunk nor any misled nonplayers give this particular dark play its "kick"; but the reactions, or mood-signs, that permeate the boundaries between play and reality do charge the event with energy. Again and again, administrators of E15M have urged me to "just wait till the assembly— then you're really going to see those kids cry!" The dynamics revealed by such comments are not cruel, I think, but rather consensual, with adults and students collaborating in the manufacturing of drama. Simply lecturing students doesn't work, one principal told the *Boston Globe,* discussing his Massachusetts school's 1996 program. "You need the details of the hospital, the ambulance, the embarrassment, the guilt, the pain, the suffering, to really drive the point home." The newspaper article described a "drunk driver" smeared with ketchup wailing as police handcuffed her. "While a few students giggled nervously, most stood in rapt silence," wrote the reporter (Nealon 1996).

Dark play "only occasionally demands make-believe," states Schechner (1988, 14), but E15M contradicts this theory. When a community stages the simulated tragedy, everyone is a player in some respect (whether passive,

active, or commenting), aware that the proceedings are drama and not reality; in this respect, they recognize and share the play frame. But the frame
is neither stable nor clearly marked. Adaptable and resilient, E15M allows
room for people to be playful in subversive, disruptive ways. No scholarly
analysis should ignore or deny what Schechner calls "the permeating, erup-
tive/disruptive energy and mood below, behind, and to the sides of focused
attention" (18). Researching this book has convinced me that such mutterings are a natural and inevitable part of play and of folk drama.

Much of the literature on play (for example, in the field of child development) has focused on its functionalist aspects, as progress or preparation
for life. But "not all play is adaptive or progressive," Mechling reminds us
(2000, 366). We can reach no illuminating insight on E15M without recognizing and accepting its dark play, including its potential for paradoxical
effects that could be dark and destructive.

From the time I began my study of Every 15 Minutes, I have been
impressed by the attention lavished on the Living Dead: the glowing eulogies, the obituaries posted in the school foyer, the gravestones erected in
the courtyard, and the flood of tears shed by peers and loved ones in genuine or contrived display. Shouldn't we wonder whether teenagers with
real problems, suffering real isolation and depression, might resent all this
attention? Most of the Living Dead tend to be students who already get
their share of strokes: they are "student leaders," "role models" or, at the
very least, kids whose parents have agreed to participate in the program,
which likely indicates a certain level of caring and involvement. The adults
expect all the kids in the audience to be "grieving"; but what if they are
quietly fuming, wishing *they* could be dead (for pretend, or even for real)
and get all this attention?

In dark play there is a kind of compulsive appeal, not unlike the urge to
pick a scab—yet scholars have largely failed to recognize this human impulse
or give it the attention it calls for. Researchers instead have ignored or denied
the phenomenon; Lindquist, for example, writes, "It is difficult to imagine
playful mourning, playful endurance of pain, or playful dying. Common
sense suggests that suffering and play are uneasy bedfellows" (2001, 14). I
disagree, especially in light of the growing taste for dark play in American
culture, from the graphic scare tactics of evangelical folk dramas like Hell
Houses to role-playing games on the Internet that fulfill people's desire to
"play" real-world problems. Indeed, soon after September 11, 2001, a *New
York Times* article chronicled the controversy over an online role-playing

game based on the World Trade Center attacks, called *9-11 Survivor,* which depicted businessmen burning to death and jumping from skyscrapers, and which provoked an outcry for "exploiting a tragedy" (Mirapaul 2003).

Interactive computer simulations have long found success in mass distribution by drawing on violent real-life conflicts such as World War II and Vietnam. But in recent years, many game developers (both corporate and independent) have pushed the limits of conventionally acceptable violence, sometimes claiming their games are socially relevant and necessary. *Waco Resurrection,* a game developed by Eddo Stern and his "Team Waco" in 2004, allows the player to "enter the mind and form of a resurrected David Koresh" and defend his cult against government assault, while recruiting followers by "radiating charisma." According to Stern's description, this game intends to reexamine the clash of worldviews, address the dynamics of the media event surrounding the tragedy, and reevaluate "the role of religion in society" (http://eddostern.com/waco_resurrection.html, accessed December 2009).

In 2006, the video game company Rockstar Games (creator of the controversial *Grand Theft Auto* series) released a video game called *Bully* in which disaffected boarding school students torment each other while negotiating the rigid social caste system. The weapons used by the protagonist to exact revenge against the school bullies are generally nonlethal (slingshots, firecrackers, stink bombs). While *Bully* has been reviled by psychologists and educators for glamorizing violence in a school setting, Rockstar Games has defended it as potentially helpful in modeling social network building skills for students (Silverman 2007; Breznican 2006).

The infamous Columbine High School massacre in 1999 has inspired several online imitations in which players may "attack monstrous incarnations of bullies and other adolescent demons" (Mirapaul 2003). Most famously, Danny Ledonne's *Super Columbine Massacre RPG* appeared in 2005 to a major outcry, documented in his 2008 film *Playing Columbine.* On his website (http://columbinegame.com, accessed December 2009), Ledonne defends his graphic simulation of school-based mass murder, claiming it "implores introspection" among players who "discuss the game's social implications in a broader context." He writes that his role-playing game "dares us into a realm of grey morality with nuanced perspectives of suffering, vengeance, horror, and reflection . . . At the end of the day, the understanding of the Columbine school shooting is deepened and redefined." He goes on to quote the poet and philosopher Bertolt Brecht: "In the dark times, will there also be singing? Yes, there will be singing about the dark times."

Disturbing but fascinating, the instinct for dark play seems to hold a powerful force in American folklore events that, with unflagging enthusiasm, exploit and publicize a growing range of shocking scenarios as material for interactive entertainment. "If you live near Stubbeman Avenue and hear gunfire this morning, don't panic—it's a simulated shooting scenario and hostage situation at North High School," announced an Oklahoma newspaper in 2003 ("It's a Drill"). In Pasco, Washington, "a dozen high school students with simulated injuries were sprawled near the tipped bus" in a school bus crash drill featuring an overturned bus and smashed car (Lord 2003). A Fremont, California, school simulated the aftermath of an earthquake to better prepare for the next one; its students were made up with fake wounds and pretended to be injured by falling debris and overturned furniture. The district newsletter informed readers that students "embrace the spirit of the drills . . . Those who are assigned to create some simulated chaos do their jobs well. Actors scream in pain as rescue workers attend them, fellow students wail with grief as they learn a classmate has died and students try to sneak off campus to test security measures" (Leatherman 2000).

Just weeks before an Every 15 Minutes event I documented in Indiana, the school staged a mock hostage drill, using kids from the drama club (one acted out the role of the gunman) as well as a gaggle of mothers who rushed screaming down the hallways. In Bucks County, Pennsylvania, the first "terrorism camp" for teens made a successful debut in summer 2003; campers spent their days practicing the arts and crafts of weaponry and intelligence in preparation for the next terrorist crisis. By 2009, the coeducational Boy Scouts Explorers program had adopted the concept at law-enforcement camps across the country; a *New York Times* feature described adolescents at a post in Imperial, California, acting out "border violence" scenarios, including illegal immigrants and disgruntled veterans wreaking destruction with pellet guns and poisonous gas. A sheriff's deputy running the program revealed a significant element of moral indoctrination to this training exercise: "This is about being a true-blooded American . . . it fits right in with the honor and bravery of the Boy Scouts." In various simulations, the Explorers respond to bus hijackings, raid marijuana fields, and thwart drug and human smugglers. The organizers strive for authenticity, and the Scouts savor it; "I like shooting [the guns]," said a sixteen-year-old girl. "I like the sound they make. It gets me excited" (Steinhauer 2009). Just outside this frame of violent play, the dads of some of the Scouts grill burgers to feed the young law enforcers.

Clark County, Washington, prides itself on its "comprehensive, all-hazards approach to school safety" (Reed 2007). High school teachers and principals from the nine school districts there convene yearly at a "training summit" to practice for a school shooting. A local newspaper offered the play-by-play (Blesch 2003): "[Two teachers], both big guys, ran in with fake guns, yelling. The principals hit the floor. 'My teacher is failing me and not giving me a chance to make up work,' improvised [one of the shooters] . . . In between acts, SWAT officers dropped the guns to their sides to free hands for coffee and pastries . . . Principals acted out parent profiles ranging from sullen and quiet to drunk and enraged."

With their contrasting images of leisure and carnage, these staged scenarios are particularly vivid examples of frame switching. Participants not only step back and forth between the multiple frames that are braided and embedded throughout the events, they seamlessly incorporate more than one at a time into their activities. Performances of the adaptable play *Bang Bang You're Dead* (mentioned in chapter 2) allow students to collaboratively build on a script that brings the details of their own lives to the fictionalized scenario onstage. In some cases, teenagers cast as characters in the play have revealed and addressed their own issues of violence and alienation through its preparation and performance (Shea 2002), using the dark material of their personal troubles to engage in imaginative public play.

Scholars from various disciplines, writing on topics from bullfighting to virtual gaming, have recognized the instinct for dark play. Anthropologist Maria-Inés Arratia has analyzed bullfighting as ritual, showing that as a subject of intellectual and political debate, it is a "most dramatic representation of the life/death dichotomy" (1988, 282), and relating it to Spain's "underlying sense of tragedy" and traditional cult of the dead. Calling them important motivators for matadors, Arratia describes the climactic gestures of the ritual, where the fighter asks for the audience's approval, presenting himself to the public so they can judge whether he deserves honor and esteem (289).

Educators and anthropologists noticed children pretend-playing with the topic of the September 11 terrorist attacks. "Play about death or any other controversial topic is typically avoided in school, but children sing and act out stories and dramas about such topics all the time," writes Anna Richman

Beresin, a professor of folklore and psychology. "We play with what disturbs us and some onlookers find the play disturbing" (2002, 332, 334).

Psychologists who study controversial forms of children's play have observed that in aggressive games, "children have valid and various reasons for playing even those games, and that they play them in different ways and with different implications for their social relations" (Schousboe 1999, 175). The variety of testimonies I collected from both teenagers and adults in Every 15 Minutes sheds light on some of the many captivating aspects of dark play, from its license to act outside normally prescribed limits to its resonance with deep and destructive human impulses to the ineffable appeal of its fun. Comments posted by students on the Every15Minutes. com Guestbook hint at such spontaneous responses:

> Quite frankly, it scared the hell out of me! It was a lot of hard work, and very time consuming, but everything came together like it was suppose to, and the whole school bonded, and it was a great thing to see guys cry, and let their emotions out. (Indiana, July 16, 2002)

> It was the most realistic freak accident that has been played out that I've ever seen . . . The program is awesome! I cried through the whole thing. Two of my good friends were in the program and I cried so hard. Casey McDonald was the drunk driver and he is like my best friend ever! I love you Casey! haha. But this program was so realistic and was the best program ever! keep it up! I hope many people got the feeling and experience I did! (Alabama, April 15, 2002)

As students gaze at their portraits and obituaries posted in the school lobby, read the glowing tributes to their lives, and smell the flowers heaped on their doorsteps by "grieving" friends, who could blame them for relishing their moment in the spotlight?

Every 15 Minutes has found its bliss in contemporary American culture—and it shares some ingredients with other emerging phenomena that incorporate drama and dark play. As a twenty-four-hour media onslaught heightens people's anxiety through alarming reports, I see the folk responding creatively and theatrically to perceived threats from all sides. It is not surprising that both youth and adults are playing with what disturbs them; in educational settings especially, the stage is open and waiting. Aspiring heroes, imagined victims, and pranksters and pirates too: all may find satisfying opportunities and rewards in these performances.

6

Shattering Frames
The Crash through YouTube's Window

WHEN EVERY 15 MINUTES WAS A YOUNG PROGRAM, it was carried by word of mouth from school to school, its emerging traditions passed on among friends and colleagues who knew each other through personal and workplace networks. Local and sometimes national newspapers and television stations put the occasional spotlight on the Grim Reaper and the Living Dead, so improbably macabre in their high school settings. But as E15M matures, its adolescence is taking place in a far more complicated media landscape.

I conducted much of the fieldwork on Every 15 Minutes between 1999 and 2003, when teenagers had fewer outlets to publicly express their views and perform for a wide audience. But in a significant shift around 2005 (when YouTube and other video-sharing sites were launched), teenagers became known for compulsively documenting their lives through photos and videos taken with their cell phones, then posting them online, where others view and post comments about them. This new norm and genre revolutionized youth culture, as teenagers quickly became fluent with the means of video production and claimed a starring role in the participatory social media of the new millennium.

High school rituals in the age of YouTube are porous events, with surrounding discourses that do not really end—they are replayed, rethought, reinterpreted, reexperienced. As I pointed out in my study of high school proms and their emerging online video archive, adolescents now take for granted their status as subjects to be publicly exhibited and commented on; in fact, many seek out this spotlight (Miller 2010). They also may take a more cynical view toward media spectacle, and make their own sense of

DOI:10.7330/9780874218923.c06   117

its meaning. Local news still covers the gripping spectacle, repeating the familiar clichés (and misinformed statistics), but now many young people are not just *in* the spotlight but also agents of it as they collaborate in the distribution of their images through online video. They participate in their own self-display; YouTube is not just a lens through which they record and watch each other, but a tool with which they can add to the dominant discourse about their generation.

My observations of Every 15 Minutes have highlighted the degree to which people relish the attention they receive when they take part in this very public event. Teenagers, of course, commonly crave attention, but it may seem that in today's multiplatform media carnival they place a higher value on celebrity than in the era before the twenty-four-hour infotainment culture. Jake Halpern, in *Fame Junkies* (2006), cites a 2005 *Washington Post*/Kaiser Family Foundation/Harvard University survey that found that 31 percent of teenagers think they will become famous one day. The current high school generation seems to continually expose its personal experiences to the world through YouTube, Facebook, Twitter, spontaneously uploading the dramas of daily life via increasingly advanced mobile devices. As in the past, being in the news is an ideal vehicle to achieve celebrity. Now, however, professional and amateur video bleed together as "news," and the distinction is irrelevant for teenagers who applaud and mock each other on video-sharing sites. In breaking down the previous boundaries between scripted and spontaneous, YouTube has also changed the nature of folk drama.

Teenagers growing up in an age of participatory media seem to accept the online video dimension of their peer culture; they incorporate these videos into the narratives that bond them socially. This new form of digital storytelling dismisses borders of time and space, and adds to the intricacy of the intersecting, overlapping frames in an event such as Every 15 Minutes.

In this chapter I present a selection of comments culled from the growing archive of YouTube videos documenting Every 15 Minutes programs across the United States. The comments reflect many of the same reactions and themes that I discovered through my firsthand observations of live events. But YouTube's lens adds yet another ambiguous frame, further complicating analysis of this multilayered phenomenon. Now we can observe a multivocal audience performing for an online community, disconnected from the real-time context and from contact with the events' original participants. While interpretations of commenters' tone, intent, and meaning thus become more difficult than ever, new opportunities also arise. YouTube gives voice to a folk critique generated by the teenage audiences typically silenced in educational and media institutions. This folk critique takes place away from E15M's physical setting, where the pressure of power relationships (among teachers, officials, parents, and peers) may inhibit expression. Instead, the anonymity and free-for-all environment of YouTube allows for a wide-ranging discourse through which we see honest reactions to various aspects of the program, and we can identify certain folk criteria by which the viewers judge the program's impact and value.

ACCELERATED TRANSMISSION

YouTube has brought into being a new form of oral transmission, expanding our previous notions of "word of mouth." In the comments posted below videos of local versions of Every 15 Minutes, one can see that participants in different schools are often surprised to find that they were not the first and only ones to create this staged drama (for example, "cool your school does it too i thought we were the only one"). In addition, YouTube comments offer some evidence that interaction between viewers may accelerate the spread of the program. Student interest appears to be one factor that can drive the spread of the program from school to school, although frustration with adult control surfaces. Some commenters ask how they can convince their own school administrators to adopt E15M; others discuss strategies to fund the production. ("Our principle says she doesnt have enough time to put this together. Its bs. I had a best friend die from a drunk-driving accident. We are making a petition to do this.")

Comments also refer to changes in the program over time, describing previous versions, often from the point of view of organizers who have produced it year after year. "We try to improve our storytelling every year," explained one YouTube poster who basked in positive viewer feedback on his E15M video. "Finding ways to use the Reaper without making it silly is a tough one." One student posted on several videos from different schools, requesting advice on "what injuries to use or crash site scenarios" for her school's program: "We don't want to use the same ones as 3 years ago." Someone responded helpfully, "I would say the 'through the windshield' seems to really catch everyone's attention and hopefully drives the point home."

"IS THIS REAL?"

Every 15 Minutes, as a form of folk drama, already presents us with ambiguous frames of belief and reality. The addition of YouTube's mediated frame complicates the task of interpretation for scholars and for participants alike. Merrill Kaplan (2010) has studied a similar phenomenon: videos of "ghost sightings" have sprung up on YouTube, creating a new genre of online ghost-story telling in which the audience participates in lively discourse concerning the authenticity of the event portrayed. Arguments over whether the videos are staged or spontaneous (based on clues in the video narrative filmed by the original poster) overlap with debates over whether ghosts exist. In these conversations, frames of credulity and incredulity are hard for the researcher to mark; they fade in and out like the blurry apparitions on film that may or may not provide evidence of haunting. An understanding of belief, or even documenting the practice of belief, has become more elusive for folklorists who do fieldwork on YouTube.

Among the comments below E15M videos, I have noticed frequent attempts by viewers to figure out what frame the action belongs in:

Did they actually die?

wait i dont get it. why would people cry if they knew this was fake?

Did Tina really die or is she part of the program? cuz i think i used to know her ???? . . . wait . . . i dont understand . . . these people didnt really die did they?

As with Kaplan's online ghost story audiences, E15M viewers engage each other in discussion over what is real and whether it matters. These three examples illustrate such dialogues:

Omg this is so sad. I go to the school across the street. Even though I didn't know these people, this brought tears to my eyes

and why is that, is their acting that good?

ha. Yeah I know its fake. But still, its good:)

is this real

are the people in the pictures dead???

if I said that it was real, would it impact you more??

This is all mock, nobody was actually injured, killed, or arrested. all of the participating students are alive and well!!

Shut up it still tramatic!!!!!!!!!!!!!!!!!!!!!

Commenters also may relate anecdotes illustrating the ubiquitous frame shifting between real and pretend in E15M:

We had our accident today, it was really sad. But then half-way through it some fat bald guy came jogging through and totally interrupted the whole thing.

My sister told me about that fat guy running and she said that the guy was going towards the firemen and asking what happened haha

We had ours at College Park High School today! It was touching . . . some lady fainted as it got too emotional for her (Due to an incident with drunk driver and her son). And they actually ended up really using one of the emergency vehicles to transport her.

Awesome video . . . My school is doing that this april . . . but at least this time they told us it was a set up . . . when my brother went to my school, they didn't say it was fake, and everyone flipped out . . . some kids needed therapy, even.

I wish they put the part where the fire truck accidently started shooting water into the sophomore crowd and the firemen had to "stop saving the kids" and stop the water from dowsing every kid in the stands.

UNSILENCED CRITICS

During the real-life proceedings of Every 15 Minutes, dissenting talk among students is shut down by those in charge. YouTube comments on E15M videos, however, freely and explicitly express criticisms of the program. Some viewers acknowledged the valuable message of the production, but were turned off by its incongruously theatrical special effects:

> The only thing that kinda ruined it though was the grim reaper dude, everyone thought that he was so stupid and it kind of ruined the feel you know?

> It just seems a little bit too "Twilight Zone."

> I don't think that the Death at the site is necessary. I mean, to me it feels like it makes it more comical.

Some criticized the scenario as unrealistic. ("Someone was drunk 8 o clock in the morning? or coming back from a rave?") To some, the lack of serious realism turned it into a joke that bordered on the offensive. ("This is cheesy as hell and the rap-rave music makes it seem like a joke. Drunk driving isn't funny and this video is a serious mockery of what it's trying to deter.") Many clearly were not buying into what they considered a waste of time:

> God we have to do this again this year!:(

> We just had this stupid thing at my school, it's so boring and fake. The only thing I learned was to not let women drive because both of the drivers were women.

> That day sucked. i was forced along with all the other seniors and juniors to stand out there and watch it. damn wind blew road dust in my freakn face. Boring

> Wow that was pathetic . . . this video is school propaganda. I hope all the parents reading this don't buy into the BS.

Even those who did express allegiance to the program also noticed and referred to their skeptical peers:

my school in wisconsin did this. i was a part of it. that was the most emotional thing i have EVER done. 95% of people did not take it seriously.

Every junior and senior at my school thought this was a joke the first day. Even I did. The second day though was really rough. Almost everyone broke into tears that day. But even the second day people just laughed at the act.

Some commenters critiqued the program's approach and rhetoric as manipulative:

This is fake.

NO SHIT.

No i meant the "every 15 min" thing, thats a lie.

I'm the girl in the video, and that's not me crying in the hospital scene. It's my mom. I was trying not to laugh the entire time (as was my dad). She was genuinely upset by the whole thing and she wasn't faking it. I, on the other hand, didn't want to do this in the first place. This video is the bane of my existence and I hate that it's on youtube.

FOLK CRITERIA AND THE CRASH

Looking beyond the outright objections voiced in the YouTube forum, we can also find a sort of folk critique being generated in the chorus of comments on how E15M is shaped and executed. The aesthetics of costume and location, the talent of the role-players, and the adherence to shared rules for the performance, as well as the quality of the video, are subject to scrutiny. As an imagined community of young critics comes together to create a conversation around each video, its members form a popular appropriation, or a folk version, of what was originally an adult-dominated narrative. The viewers' remarks also establish an in-group standard of critique for various productions' aesthetics, which may be praised or pilloried.

This one is the BEST it has the best car crash scene ever!!!!

This is as crappy as it gets . . . u put nothing into it . . . at least make it realistic. 10 mph collision doesn't = 4 deaths

I had mine today it was really good it actually showed the drunk kids and the dead body was really bloody, and the cars were totaled but it was in our football stadium, so it killed the mood

Ours was pathetic. They had the crash staged on the football field, so fake.

I thought it was entertaining that the truck was crushed as if it had been rolled over, yet the car just had a compressed hood.

While a good deal of snarky sniping occurs, this critical community also takes the performative aspect of the play seriously—on its own terms as an event worthy of interest and appraisal. All the theatrical trappings of the program provide material for critique:

My school just did this last week. It wasn't as good as this one with all the make-up but it was still very emotional and definately made an impact.

I think the makeup was a bit too much? but everybody did good in this video (:

It was a good video for part one but the slow music at the crash site scene just really kills the suspense

the vid is good, but it's way too much like the 07 version, shoulda changed up the music a little more

The acting, too, comes under the critical lens, sometimes with an ironic or teasing overtone since the actors are untrained amateurs enlisted from the ranks:

That look seriously unrehearsed, it was kinda of messy and the cop was like "do I go in now?"

The fire fighters weren't very enthusiastic . . . aren't they supposed to be able to get their gear on in like 45 seconds or something . . . they weren't even running to the truck . . . I mean come on

I need more emotion from dead guy #2, i mean hes dead but im just not feeling it. Jazz hands people! Jazz hands!!!

Cool having the dead guy sit up and talk.

Obnoctious . . . that girl overdid it a little on the screaming.

A competitive or envious tone often creeps into the commentary:

my school did this waaayyyy better

damn ur make up and program is soooo much better than ours

man, northgate gets steadycams? we don't get those.

[My school] sucked compared to these ones the acting sucked in mine.

theres not really much emotion in this . . . you need the real emotions . . . our skool had the parents go to the hospital, morgue and the jail . . . it was very emotional, there was real tears . . . the doctor in the hospital even cried . . . im not trying to dog you guys . . . you guys did good.

Wow, you guys had so much goin for yah. Bet you had a lot more time than us. We had horrible actors half a week to shoot and edit prolouge and 12 hours to shoot and edit crash,hostpital and notifications. I also notive u had a boom and steady cam. Don't know why we didnt use ours, o wait i remember the administration f'd us and we had to time to plan anything. O dude you guy were allowed to go in the chopper not cool. They made me stand like 20 feet from the chopper.

THROWING ROCKS AT THE FRAME

As I have shown in previous chapters, even participants who are engrossed in the proceedings still may step in and out of the *play* or *pretend* frame as Every 15 Minutes unfolds. But not everyone who participates in the event willingly enters the frame at all. Hecklers are quickly disciplined if they speak too loudly in school, but online they unleash their hostility and derision. Their commentary is often at the expense of the proceedings: insolent wise-cracks that shatter the frame like rocks hurled at YouTube's window.

too bad kids are stubborn and dont give a fuck . . . im gonna go have a drink

Think u guys have some problems . . . the guy who got killed was my friend and he owed me like 87 dollars for a date

how cool is it to be in jail.

this is the funniest shit ever

ur mom puts out every fifteen minutes

Don't drink and drive. You might spill your drink.

if you had johny cochran you'd had gotten off the hook

the message is unclear but i think i got it: women shouldn't be allowed to drive?

drink drivin is a sport where I'm from homie.

This video makes me thirsty.

i got in a car with a drunk driver the night this happend ha sorry bud

People may dismiss this Internet "trash talk," but we can learn from it. The hecklers' emergent and irreverent expressions subvert the dominant discourse and reveal its fault lines. They give us insight that we cannot get from attending the public event, no matter how intently we watch and listen. It may seem to sweep everyone up, but actually it involves a vast complexity of individual perceptions and responses.

Although Internet fieldwork is limited and lacking in context, it serves as an essential ethnographic method in the study of ritualesque (Santino 2009) collective experiences. YouTube can be a cacophonous online auditorium, and here the high school students of E15M assemble and speak out on their own terms. Their folk critique as well as their mordant jeers exemplify this, as videos are endorsed or repudiated on terms meaningful to the participants and the viewers. A new level of discussion surfaces because the life of the event is extended as it is replayed online. Just as the new media context is changing many traditional adolescent rites of passage, it is also a significant development in the new tradition of staged tragedy.

Conclusion

Rustles in the Gallery

As the service proceeded, the clergyman drew such pictures of the graces, the winning ways, and the rare promise of the lost lads that every soul there, thinking he recognized these pictures, felt a pang in remembering that he had persistently blinded himself to them always before and had as persistently seen only faults and flaws in the poor boys. The minister related many a touching incident in the lives of the departed, too, which illustrated their sweet, generous natures, and the people could easily see, now, how noble and beautiful those episodes were, and remembered with grief that at the time they occurred they had seemed rank rascalities, well deserving of the cowhide. The congregation became more and more moved, as the pathetic tale went on, till at last the whole company broke down and joined the weeping mourners in a chorus of anguished sobs, the preacher himself giving way to his feelings and crying in the pulpit.

There was a rustle in the gallery, which nobody noticed; a moment later the church door creaked; the minister raised his streaming eyes above his handkerchief, and stood transfixed! First one and then another pair of eyes followed the minister's, and then almost with one impulse the congregation rose and stared while the three dead boys came marching up the aisle . . . They had been hid in the unused gallery listening to their own funeral sermon!

*Aunt Polly, Mary, and the Harpers threw themselves upon their restored ones, smothered them with kisses and poured out thanksgivings . . . Suddenly the minister shouted at the top of his voice: "Praise God from whom all blessings flow—*SING!*—and put your hearts in it!"*

And they did. "Old Hundred" swelled up with a triumphant burst, and while it shook the rafters Tom Sawyer the Pirate looked around upon the envying juveniles about him and confessed in his heart that this was the proudest moment of his life.

—Mark Twain, *The Adventures of Tom Sawyer*

Today teenagers all across America are acting out bloody scenarios of violence and death, as their teachers, parents, and mentors look on

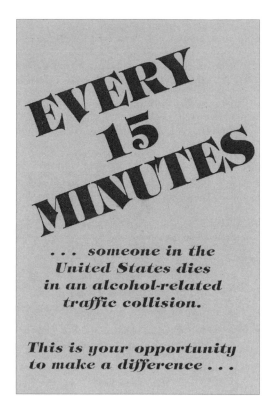

in tearful approval. Each year, under the banner of the various programs discussed in this book, more teenagers bleed and expire. They reenact fatal car accidents and attend their own mock funerals; they burst down hallways with machine guns and hold their classmates hostage; they scream under the knife in simulated botched Hell House abortions. Events are staged with great care and great gusto, along a spectrum from drill to elaborate narrative. As educational institutions (both religious and secular) place increasing faith in dramatic methods as a means to teach a lesson, to transform attitudes, and to inspire good behavior, Every 15 Minutes and its cousins have hit their stride in American culture.

Jay Mechling, who has called for scholars of play to engage in more discourse around matters of morality, has rejected in his essay "Morality Play" (1989a) the notion that play is amoral, or an arbitrary realm in which people collectively participate without moral responsibility. Mechling is not the only one to raise such questions; Gary Alan Fine's 1991 piece "Justifying Fun: Why We Do Not Teach Exotic Dance in High School" notes that people, conscious of the public stereotypes attached to their forms of expression and folklore, attempt to "give value to their playful desires" and legitimize play as productive and meaningful, using "instrumental rationales." Fine notes that a group's playful activity might provoke "special feelings of a highly moral and almost religious intensity" and that participants use a "finely spun rhetoric" to justify their fun as a moral enterprise, although to the uninitiated it might seem bizarre (87–88).

Naturally, a folk drama based on drunk driving and death is loaded with issues of morality and community values; and even after years of soaking in the bloody lessons of Every 15 Minutes, I still find something uniquely bizarre in each new enactment. Participants in this drama are perfectly aware of its ambiguity, its dark and playful paradox. Their concern over drunk driving, and their motivation to bring the community together behind a worthy cause, may at times provide "the garb of a calling" (Fine 1991, 98) to disguise how much morbid fun they are having. On the other hand, I see a valuable perspective in the Huizinga (1950) notion of play as separate from "wisdom and folly, truth and falsehood, good and evil" (6). The educational and moral goals of E15M, perhaps evident on the surface, do not necessarily infuse the experience of all participants. Instead, players contribute to the action as unique, contradictory individuals, harboring their own interpretations and pulled by their own callings.

Still, Mechling is right: the study of play and its moral nature can lead to new insights about what is really going on in an event such as E15M. We should use these insights to raise questions that do have moral importance in our contemporary culture, and also have implications for educators, psychologists, sociologists, and other thoughtful folk. Where are the boundaries between real and perceived trauma? Why are so many teenagers, and adults as well, desperate for attention? How does our educational system recognize and respond to this need? How are we adapting and contributing to a culture of media exhibitionism, with teenage killers on magazine covers, compulsive television coverage of freeway car chases, and an entertainment industry gripped by reality shows?

These questions may be disturbing, as they shine a spotlight on the dark side of play's appeal; yet they must be raised, because they are about a very human element in our contemporary folklore. As Mechling observes, it's not about judging this human element, but about recognizing its relationship to a world in which tragedies and cruelty do exist.

When a form of leisure involves such morally controversial material, it seems natural that participants would feel compelled to justify it, as Fine has observed with cockfighting (1992) and Olmsted with gun collectors (1988). Those who enjoy dark play may self-consciously defend their activities as character building, especially when they must negotiate the surrounding politics and economics (Fine 1992, 249–250). In the face of social criticism and limited resources, people must have strong motivations to persevere, notes Fine. Clearly E15M enthusiasts, for individual as well as communal reasons, are having enough fun producing this dark drama to make the cost and trouble worth it (though they may repeat the mantra that the reward is "even one life saved"). E15M does not just spread by itself; it takes commitment and energy from people willing to fight for its moral and practical justification. "We are criticized for supporting it, even sometimes in the press. Every dollar of SDFS [Safe and Drug Free Schools] money must go to support programs that have been proven to be effective, and some people are critical of the program—it has never been evaluated," said a drug education program coordinator I interviewed. Speaking (as many administrators do) of the need for community "buy-in" to back the program, she emphasized that to get people involved and excited "the drama *is* important!"

George Ratliff, director of the 2001 documentary *Hell House,* spoke on National Public Radio's *Weekend Edition* in August 2002 about the highly motivated evangelists who act out the scenes of horror in their haunted houses:

> It really, really is the most exciting time of the year for them—they look forward to it all year round—and the time of the year that they save the most souls or bring the biggest number of people into the church. And also, it's fun. You know, the kids—this is the one time they get to dance in a rave scene or they get to play a drunk or a drug user or they act out sex scenes and things like that. These are things that they never get to at least openly play out, and they get to do it under the auspices of doing it as work one time of the year, and they really love it.

Promoters may not be able to justify their fun and effort with scientific proof that they have saved souls in the church or saved lives on the highway. But there are all kinds of proof, and all kinds of perceptions as to what success means. From the Cal State Chico study referenced in chapter 2 to the predictable hyperbolic claim "There wasn't a dry eye in the auditorium," organizers are interpreting E15M as a success. And for many participants, satisfaction may have more to do with fun—in whatever form they find it. (As I have illustrated, fun has many vehicles here—attention, vacation from school, creativity, excitement, and the fun "for its own sake.") For a couple of days, E15M makes school more fun than usual. "I'm in home school and we don't get to do stuff like this," wrote one Guestbook visitor, with a perceptible shade of envy.

Every 15 Minutes events are, like the beauty pageants studied by Lavenda, "complex, layered performances that are continually being interpreted and reinterpreted" (1991, 166). Lavenda alludes to "reflexive outcomes," by which he implies that people's interpretation of the goal of the event serves as a guide for making judgments about it. Adult and student E15M participants in the high schools I visited are acutely aware of each other and their impact on each other, and they are trying to fit in to community criteria for judging. However, their individual responses to E15M cannot be generalized.

The two teachers quoted below, the first in rural New Mexico and the second in urban Los Angeles, both came to ambivalent conclusions about E15M's effectiveness at preventing drunk driving:

> From what I've seen in my area, it has made an impact. There are still those few kids that have their disbelief . . . they know it's all fake . . . They're not accepting the fact that that's really what's going to happen. They think, "Oh, they're just trying to scare us." But the ones that were actually in the program, the kids that they used, I think it has impacted them. Over the last year, I haven't seen as many teens out, you know—but of course, they could be hiding. You never know where they're at or what they're doing.

> Many of the kids who are doing this, in fact the majority of the kids that are doing it, were the ones who were out driving around Saturday night after the prom [the following weekend]. These are all the party animals, playing the dead people. They're having a good old time today.

A Colorado student who played a crash victim in the mock accident wrote her mixed impressions on the E15M Guestbook message board in September 2002: "It impacted almost the whole school . . . for a few days. I'm not saying that this program's not effective because it really is. It's just that the people in my school are too thick headed and ignorant to learn what's good for them . . . People say that if we just reach one person it'll all be worth it. It might be worth it for a while but think of how many people will just take that information and blow it out the window."

Yet two hours earlier that same day, a parent with two kids participating in the same town's program posted a contrasting description in the Guestbook:

"It was an emotional rollercoster for 2 days. It delivered a great message and I believe it made an impact on the whole student body." And five days earlier, a teacher from the very same school had posted this comment: "Awesome program. I believe this made a huge impact on our students."

Participants not only perceive things through multiple lenses, they express those perceptions in response to ever-emerging situational contexts. In one striking example, a Maryland student talking to a newspaper reporter in the presence of her friends referred to being "roped into talking to a grief counselor," but later, when asked by the police coordinator if she was okay, she replied, "Oh, yes, we got to talk to the counselor," giving the impression that the talk had been therapeutic.

The newspaper article the next day wasn't as preoccupied with ambiguity as I have been. Describing the Grim Reaper's visit to a classroom, the reporter wrote, "The giggling stopped. Mouths were agape and the teacher stood speechless. After a few moments, one student whispered, 'Somebody say something, please.' It is exactly the effect organizers want the program to have" (Hedgpeth 2001).

The full picture is much more complicated and conflicting. A Maine student's Guestbook comment in May 2002 reflects this: "'Every 15 Minutes' changed part of our school but to some kids in our school they thought of it as a joke and didn't think it would change their mind . . . It was disgusting in some ways and touching in others. Just to see the caskets laying in the middle of our gym was amazing. Please bring the program back!!!!!"

Even amid sarcastic comments—"I see dead people," one student droned, quoting from the hit horror movie *The Sixth Sense*—people tend to see what they choose to see and block out the mutterings. A teacher attested on an E15M website that "there were tears all around, and although some were still laughing by the end, it was nervous laughter. You could tell they were affected, and I can imagine that they went home and cried."

As we have seen in chapter 6, comments posted on YouTube videos of E15M events sometimes attest to what does happen when the program is over and the students go home, and the mixed, mediated emotional signals can confound our attempts to make meaning from the dramatic event.

Educator James Herndon, in *How to Survive in Your Native Land* (1971), has eloquently evoked the futility of discerning and interpreting what plays out behind the curtains of the high school scene—the "hidden transcripts," as I (borrowing Sutton-Smith's term) call them. Herndon writes:

As long as you can threaten people, you can't tell whether or not they really want to do what you are proposing that they do. You can't tell if they are inspired by it, you can't tell if they learn anything from it, you can't tell if they would keep on doing it if you weren't threatening them.

You cannot tell. You cannot tell if the kids want to come to your class or not. You can't tell if they are motivated or not. You can't tell if they learn anything or not. All you can tell is, they'd rather come to your class than go to jail.

This drunk-driving drama, its attendant emotional expressions, and its layers of ever-shifting frames unfold in a context full of power relationships, threats, moral discourse, real grieving, boredom, and hunger for attention. Amid all that, as Herndon reminds us, it's hard to tell what and whether people are really learning. Imprisoned by the tedious rules and routines of school and workplace, they might express enthusiasm simply at the prospect of escape. The E15M phenomenon puts a dark-play twist on that escape. Its players are released from obscurity and monotony into a mock ordeal in which they actually do go to jail—or to the hospital in a body bag, or to their own funerals.

Every 15 Minutes, like play itself, is multiperspective, ambiguous, paradoxical, competitive, slippery, and appealing to darker impulses that are normally considered inappropriate or dangerous. As Bateson pointed out in his landmark essay (1955), play's complexity includes opportunities for creativity, control, histrionics, and even self-pity. It engages people for reasons that are shifting, contradictory, and emotionally tangled. In the midst of a crowd apparently awed by classmates strewn on the pavement, mutterings were everywhere; an anonymous adolescent voice behind me said, "That's going to be me this weekend."

Every 15 Minutes shows us that play can be tragically horrifying and yet strangely satisfying. A ritualesque celebration of death (Santino 2009), it doesn't require that every participant be fully engrossed or ultimately transformed. It only requires that enough people have enough fun—in their own intimately complex ways—to want to invite the Reaper back next year.

Even a nurse working at the admitting desk in the hospital emergency room (where she witnesses real trauma every day) breathed an ambiguous sigh as the Living Dead victim expired in the next room: "Are they having fun? They look like they're having fun. I wish I was a part of that."

References

Abrahams, Roger D. 1986. "Play in the Face of Death: Transgression and Inversion in a West Indian Wake." In *The Many Faces of Play*, ed. Kendall Blanchard, 29–45. Champaign, IL: Human Kinetics Publishers. (In Proceedings of the 1983 Annual Meeting of the Association for the Anthropological Study of Play, Baton Rouge, LA, 11–16 February.)

Anastas, Robert. 1982. *Students Against Drunk Driving*. Marlborough, MA: S.A.D.D.

Arnett, J. 1990. "Drunk Driving, Sensation Seeking, and Egocentrism among Adolescents." *Personality and Individual Differences* 11 (6): 541–6. http://dx.doi.org/10.1016/0191-8869(90)90035-P.

Arratia, Maria-Inés. 1988. "Bullfights: Art, Sport, Ritual." *Play and Culture* 1 (3): 282–90.

Ashworth, Peter, and Ursula Lucas. 2000. "Achieving Empathy and Engagement: A Practical Approach to the Design, Conduct and Reporting of Phenomenographic Research." *Studies in Higher Education* 25 (3): 295–308. http://dx.doi.org/10.1080/713696153.

Associated Press. 2001. "'Executing' bin Laden a Hit in Haunted House." *The Associated Press*, 26 October.

Associated Press. 2002. "Staged Drunken Driving Death Irks Students." *The Associated Press*, 13 May.

Bateson, Gregory. 1955. "A Theory of Play and Fantasy." In *Psychiatric Research Reports*, 2: 39–51. New York: Ballantine Books.

Bauman, Richard, ed. 1992. *Folklore, Cultural Performances, and Popular Entertainments: A Communications-Centered Handbook*. New York: Oxford University Press.

Beckwith, Martha Warren. 1922. *Folk-Games of Jamaica*. Publications of the Folk-Lore Foundation, No. 1. New York: Vassar College.

Beresin, Anna Richman. 2002. "Children's Expressive Culture in Light of September 11, 2001." *Anthropology & Education Quarterly* 33 (3): 331–7. http://dx.doi.org/10.1525/aeq.2002.33.3.331.

Best, Joel. 2001. *Damned Lies and Statistics: Untangling Numbers from the Media, Politicians and Activists*. Berkeley: University of California Press.

Blesch, Gregg Sherrard. 2003. "Drill Readies Officials for Violence on Campuses." *The Clark County Columbian*, 14 August.

Bordin, Judy, Matthew Bumpus, and Shane Hunt. 2003. "Every 15 Minutes: A Preliminary Evaluation of a School-Based Drinking/Driving Program." *California Journal of Health Promotion* 1 (3): 1–6.

Botvin, G. J., and E. M. Botvin. 1997. "School-Based Programs." In *Substance Abuse: A Comprehensive Textbook*, 3rd ed., ed. J. H. Lowinson, P. Ruiz, R. B. Millman, and J. G. Langrod, 764–75. Baltimore: Williams and Wilkins.

Brantley, Ben. 2006. "A Guided Tour of Hell, with an Appearance by Satan." *New York Times*, 14 October, B7.

Brewster, Paul G., ed. 1952. "Children's Games and Rhymes." In *The Frank C. Brown Collection of North Carolina Folklore,* 1: 31–219. Durham, NC: Duke University Press.

Breznican, Anthony. 2006. "'Bully' Hits Schoolyard, for Good or Bad." *USA Today,* 9 August.

Caillois, Roger. 1961. *Man, Play and Games.* Glencoe, IL: Free Press.

Campbell, J. W. 1996. "Professional Wrestling: Why the Bad Guy Wins." *Journal of American Culture* 19 (2): 127–32. http://dx.doi.org/10.1111/j.1542-734X.1996.1902_127.x.

Carroll, Jon. 2008. "Trauma Techniques." *The San Francisco Chronicle,* 18 June.

CDC (Centers for Disease Control and Prevention). 2009. *Youth Risk Behavior Surveillance—United States, 2007.* Atlanta: National Center for Chronic Disease Prevention and Health Promotion.

Cohen, Deborah. 1994. "Bringing up Baby." *Education Week* 16 (November): 40.

Cohen, Patricia. 2001. "Sorry, You've Got the Wrong Number: Interview with Joel Best." *The New York Times,* 26 May.

Coles, Adrienne. 1998. "Proms, Graduations Spur Schools to Redouble Anti-Drinking Efforts." *Education Week* 17 (39): 1.

Cosentino, Donald. 1982. *Defiant Maids and Stubborn Farmers: Tradition and Invention in Mende Story Performance.* Cambridge: Cambridge University Press. http://dx.doi.org/10.1017/CBO9780511753053.

Cox, John. 1942. "Singing Games." *Southern Folklore Quarterly* 6: 183–261.

Csikszentmihalyi, Mihaly. 1975. *Beyond Boredom and Anxiety: The Experience of Play in Work and Games.* San Francisco: Jossey-Bass.

Dawson, D. A. 1992. "Professional Wrestling as Ritual Drama in American Popular Culture." *Sociology of Sport Journal* 9 (4): 423–4.

D'Emidio-Caston, M., and J. H. Brown. 1998. "The Other Side of the Story: Student Narratives on the California Drug, Alcohol, and Tobacco Education Programs." *Evaluation Review* 22 (1): 95–117. http://dx.doi.org/10.1177/0193841X9802200105. Medline:10183303.

Dewey, John. 1980 [1916]. "Democracy and Education." In *John Dewey: The Middle Works, 1899–1924,* ed. J. A. Boydston, 9: 1–402. Carbondale: Southern Illinois University Press.

Drewal, Margaret Thompson. 1992. *Yoruba Ritual: Performers, Play, Agency.* Bloomington: Indiana University Press.

Dundes, Alan. 1964. "On Game Morphology: A Study of the Structure of Non-Verbal Folklore." *New York Folklore Quarterly* 20: 276–88.

Ebersole, Gary. 2000. "The Function of Ritual Weeping Revisited: Affective Expression and Moral Discourse." *History of Religions* 39 (3): 211–46. http://dx.doi.org/10.1086/463591.

Ellis, Bill. 1981. "The Camp Mock-Ordeal: Theater as Life." *Journal of American Folklore* 94 (374): 486–505. http://dx.doi.org/10.2307/540502.

Ellis, Bill. 1996. "Legend-Trips and Satanism: Adolescents' Ostensive Traditions as 'Cult' Activity." In *New Perspectives on Contemporary Legend,* ed. Paul Smith and Gillian Bennett, 167–86. New York: Garland.

Ellis, Bill. 2001. *Aliens, Ghosts, and Cults: Legends We Live.* Jackson: University Press of Mississippi.

Emerson, R., R. Fretz, and L. Shaw. 1995. *Writing Ethnographic Fieldnotes.* Chicago: University of Chicago Press.

Erickson, Frederick. 1984. "What Makes School Ethnography 'Ethnographic'?" *Anthropology & Education Quarterly* 15 (1): 51–66. http://dx.doi.org/10.1525/aeq.1984.15.1.05x1472p.

Erikson, Erik. 1963. *Childhood and Society*. New York: Norton.

Escobedo, L. G. 1994. "Drinking and Driving among US High-School Students." *Lancet* 343 (8894): 421–2. http://dx.doi.org/10.1016/S0140-6736(94)91258-0. Medline:7905577.

Farrell, Edwin. 1988. "Giving Voice to High School Students: Pressure and Boredom, Ya Know What I'm Sayin'?" *American Educational Research Journal* 25 (4): 489–502.

Fine, Gary Alan. 1983. *Shared Fantasy: Role-Playing Games as Social Worlds*. Chicago: University of Chicago Press.

Fine, Gary Alan. 1986. "Organized Baseball and Its Folk Equivalents: The Transition from Informal to Formal Control." In *Cultural Dimensions of Play, Games, and Sport*, ed. B. Mergen, 175–90, Champaign, IL: Human Kinetics Publishers.

Fine, Gary Alan. 1991. "Justifying Fun: Why We Do Not Teach Exotic Dance in High School." *Play and Culture* 4 (2): 87–99.

Fine, Gary Alan. 1992. "The Depths of Deep Play: The Rhetoric and Resources of Morally Controversial Leisure." *Play and Culture* 5 (3): 246–51.

Furlong, M. J., J. M. Casas, C. Corral, and M. Gordon. 1997. "Changes in Substance Use Patterns Associated with the Development of a Community Partnership Project." *Evaluation and Program Planning* 20 (3): 299–305. http://dx.doi.org/10.1016/S0149-7189(97)00009-8.

Garrison, Jessica. 2000. "Skit on Drunk Driving Unsettles Students: Police Stage Report, Falsely Telling Seniors a Classmate Was Killed in Crash." *Los Angeles Times*, 7 April.

Geertz, Clifford. 1972. "Deep Play: Notes on the Balinese Cockfight." *Daedalus* 101: 1–37.

Georges, Robert A. 1969. "The Relevance of Models for Analyses of Traditional Play Activities." *Southern Folklore Quarterly* 33: 1–23.

Goffman, Erving. 1974. *Frame Analysis*. New York: Harper & Row.

Goffman, Erving. 1981. *Forms of Talk*. Philadelphia: University of Pennsylvania Press.

Goldstein, Kenneth S. 1971. "Strategy in Counting Out: An Ethnographic Folklore Field Study." In *The Study of Games*, ed. E. M. Avedon and B. Sutton-Smith, 167–78. New York: John Wiley and Sons.

Goodwin, Marjorie Harness. 1985. "The Serious Side of Jump Rope: Conversational Practices and Social Organization in the Frame of Play." *Journal of American Folklore* 98 (389): 315–30. http://dx.doi.org/10.2307/539938.

Goodwin, Marjorie Harness. 1995. "Co-Construction in Girls' Hopscotch." *Research on Language and Social Interaction* 28 (3): 261–81. http://dx.doi.org/10.1207/s15327973rlsi2803_5.

Gordon, Pat. 1999. "Seasonal Look at Reality's Horrors: On Halloween, Texas Church Uses True Stories to Attract Teenagers." *The Boston Globe*, 31 October.

Governors Highway Safety Association and Insurance Institute for Highway Safety (IIHS). May 2011. Graduated Driver Licenses (GDL) Laws. http://www.ghsa.org.

Green, Thomas A. 1978. "Toward a Definition of Folk Drama." *Journal of American Folklore* 91 (361): 843–50. http://dx.doi.org/10.2307/538679.

Greenwood, Peter W. 2005. *Changing Lives: Delinquency Prevention as Crime-Control Policy*. Chicago: University of Chicago Press.

Haines, Michael P. 1998. "Social Norms: A Wellness Model for Health Promotion in Higher Education." *Wellness Management* 14 (4): 1–8.

Halpern, Jake. 2006. *Fame Junkies: The Hidden Truths behind America's Favorite Addiction.* New York: Houghton Mifflin Harcourt.

Handelman, Don. 1977. "Play and Ritual: Complementary Frames of Meta-Communication." In *It's a Funny Thing, Humour,* ed. A. J. Chapman and H. Foot, 185–92. London: Pergamon.

Handelman, Don, and David Shulman. 1997. *God Inside Out: <S>iva's Game of Dice.* Oxford: Oxford University Press.

Hawthorne, G. 2001. "Drug Education: Myth and Reality." *Drug and Alcohol Review* 20 (1): 111–9. http://dx.doi.org/10.1080/09595230125182.

Hedgpeth, Dana. 2001. "'Every 15 Minutes' a Sobering Lesson; Drunken Driving Program Hits Home with Students." *The Washington Post,* 10 May.

Hedland, Katherine. 1994. "Mock Accident Sends Message to Students." *Moscow-Pullman Daily News,* 15 March.

Herndon, James. 1971. *How to Survive in Your Native Land.* New York: Simon and Schuster.

Hoffman, Allison. 2008. "Teachers Defend Shock Tactics in Teen Drunk Driving Program." *The Associated Press,* 13 June.

Holcomb, Jack Andrew. 2000. "Playing Popular Culture: A Folkloristic Perspective on Role-Playing Games and Gamers." PhD diss., University of Louisiana at Lafayette.

Hoyle, Susan M. 1993. "Participation Frameworks in Sportscasting Play: Imaginary and Literal Footings." In *Framing in Discourse,* ed. Deborah Tannen, 114–45. Oxford: Oxford University Press.

Hughes, Linda A. 1991. "A Conceptual Framework for the Study of Children's Gaming." *Play and Culture* 4: 284–301.

Huizinga, Johan. 1950. *Homo Ludens: A Study of the Play Element in Culture.* Boston: Beacon Press.

IIHS (Insurance Institute for Highway Safety). 2009. "Fatality Facts 2009: Teenagers." http://www.iihs.org/research/fatality_facts_2009/teenagers.html.

It's a Drill. 2003. *The Norman Transcript,* 2 July.

Jeffrey, L. P., P. Negro, D. S. Miller, and J. D. Frisone. 2003. "The Rowan University Social Norms Project." In *The Social Norms Approach to Preventing School and College Age Substance Abuse,* 100–110. San Francisco: Jossey-Bass.

Juneau, Jane Dove. 2000. "The Debate over 'Every 15 Minutes.'" *The Mammoth Times,* 18 May.

Kapferer, Judith L. 1981. "Socialization and the Symbolic Order of the School." *Anthropology & Education Quarterly* 12 (4): 258–74. http://dx.doi.org/10.1525/aeq.1981.12.4.05x1812r.

Kaplan, Merrill. 2010. "Memorates on YouTube, *or* The Legend Conduit Is a Series of Tubes." Paper presented at the annual conference of the Western States Folklore Society, Salem, OR.

Karlin, Rick. 2002. "Drama Offers Life over Tragedy, but Some Wonder If Accidents Staged to Show Drunken Driving Dangers Work." *The Times Union,* 11 May.

Katz, Matthew. 1998. "'Hell Houses' Receive Spirited—and Controversial—Reviews: Creators Defend Them as Way to Lead Teens to Salvation." *The Washington Times,* 23 October.

Klepp, Knut-Inge, Cheryl L. Perry, and David R. Jacobs. 1991. "Etiology of Drinking and Driving among Adolescents: Implications for Primary Prevention." *Health Education and Behavior* 18 (4): 415–27.

Kreft, I.G.G., and J. H. Brown, eds. 1998. *Zero Effects of Drug Prevention Programs: Issues and Solutions*. Thousand Oaks, CA: Sage Periodicals.

Lavenda, Robert H. 1988. "Minnesota Queen Pageants: Play, Fun, and Dead Seriousness in a Festive Mode." *Journal of American Folklore* 101 (400): 168–75. http://dx.doi.org/10.2307/540107.

Lavenda, Robert H. 1991. "Community Festivals, Paradox, and the Manipulation of Uncertainty." *Play and Culture* 4: 153–68.

Lavenda, Robert H. 1992. "'Passages to Play: Paradox and Process'; Response." *Play and Culture* 5 (1): 22–24.

Leaf, W. A., and D. F. Preusser. 1995. *Evaluation of Youth Peer-to-Peer Impaired Driving Programs*. Washington, DC: National Highway Traffic Safety Administration.

Leatherman, Gary. 2000. "Hopkins Marks Loma Prieta Anniversary with Disaster Drill." *Fremont Unified School District News*, 1 December.

Lesko, Nancy. 1988. *Symbolizing Society: Stories, Rites and Structure in a Catholic High School*. London: Taylor & Francis.

Lewis, George. 2001. "'Every 15 Minutes' Program at Chino High School in California Teaches Teens about Dangers of Drinking and Driving." *The Today Show*, NBC, 10 April.

Lightner, C. 1985. "Safe Rides." *Mothers Against Drunk Driving—M.A.D.D.* 8 February.

Lindquist, Galina. 2001. "Elusive Play and Its Relations to Power." *Focaal: European Journal of Anthropology* 37: 13–23.

Linkenbach, Jeff, and H. Wesley Perkins. 2005. "Montana's MOST of Us Don't Drink and Drive Campaign: A Social Norms Strategy to Reduce Impaired Driving among 21–34-Year-Olds." Washington, DC: National Highway Traffic Safety Administration. http://www.nhtsa.gov/people/injury/alcohol/SocialNorms_Strategy/images/SocialNorms.pdf.

Lobdell, William. 2000. "Aiming to Scare the Devil Out of You: Conservative Christians Are Finding Alternatives to Halloween." *The Los Angeles Times*, 27 October.

Lord, Kristina. 2003. "School Bus Drivers Prepare for Worst with Crash Drill." *Tri City Herald*, 2 July.

MacKinnon, D. P., M. A. Pentz, B. I. Broder, and M. G. MacLean. 1994. "Social Influences on Adolescent Driving under the Influence in a Sample of High School Students." *Alcohol, Drugs, and Driving* 10 (3–4): 233–41.

Magliocco, Sabina. 1985. "The Bloomington Jaycees' Haunted House." *Indiana Folklore and Oral History* 14: 19–28.

Marselas, Kimberly. 2002. "'Empathy Belly' Gives Students Vivid Feel of Pregnancy." *The Maryland Capital-Gazette*, 1 November.

Mayton, D., E. Nagel, and R. Parker. 1991. *Adolescents Who Drive under the Influence: Correlates and Risk Factors*. Washington, DC: US Department of Education.

McCarthy, John. 1990. "Field of Dreams and Dreams of Fields: Baseball Simulations as Reality and Imitation." *Play and Culture* 3: 32–43.

McGonigal, Jane. 2003. "'This Is Not a Game': Immersive Aesthetics and Collective Play." Melbourne Digital Arts and Culture conference papers: Fine Art Forum 17, no. 8. http://www.fineartforum.org.

McKnight, A. J. 1986. "Intervention in Teenage Drunk Driving." *Alcohol, Drugs and Driving: Abstracts and Reviews* 2 (1): 17–28.

Mechling, Jay. 1980. "The Magic of the Boy Scout Campfire." *Journal of American Folklore* 93 (367): 35–56. http://dx.doi.org/10.2307/540212.

Mechling, Jay. 1989a. "Morality Play." *Play and Culture* 2 (4): 304–16.

Mechling, Jay. 1989b. "'Banana Cannon' and Other Folk Traditions between Human and Nonhuman Animals." *Western Folklore* 48 (4): 312–23. http://dx.doi. org/10.2307/1499545.

Mechling, Jay. 2000. "Performing Imaginary Rhetoric." *American Quarterly* 52 (2): 364–70. http://dx.doi.org/10.1353/aq.2000.0019.

Mechling, Jay. 2008. "Gun Play." *American Journal of Play* 1 (2): 192–209.

Miller, Montana. 2010. "Taking a New Spotlight to the Prom: Youth Culture and Its Emerging Video Archive." *Journal of American Culture* 33 (1): 12–23. http:// dx.doi.org/10.1111/j.1542-734X.2010.00726.x.

Mirapaul, Matthew. 2003. "Online Games Grab Grim Reality." *The New York Times*, 17 September.

MADD (Mothers Against Drunk Driving). 2011. "Position Statements." http://www. madd.org/about-us/position-statements/madds-position-statements.html.

NCIA (National Center on Institutions and Alternatives). 1979. *Scared Straight: A Second Look*. Alexandria, VA: NCIA.

NHTSA (National Highway Traffic Safety Administration). 2001. "Alcohol and Highway Safety 2001: A Review of the State of Knowledge." http://www.nhtsa.gov/people/ injury/research/alcoholhighway/executive_summary.htm.

NHTSA (National Highway Traffic Safety Administration). 2008a. "Statistical Analysis of Alcohol-Related Driving Trends, 1982–2005." http://www.nhtsa.gov.

NHTSA (National Highway Traffic Safety Administration). 2008b. *Traffic Safety Facts 2008: Young Drivers*. Washington, DC: NHTSA.

NIAAA (National Institute on Alcohol Abuse and Alcoholism). 2011. "Alcohol and Alcohol Problems Science Database." http://etoh.niaaa.nih.gov/ (accessed June 2011).

Nealon, Patricia. 1996. "'Crash' Urges Students to Take Smarts to Prom." *The Boston Globe,* 16 May.

Newell, William Wells. 1963 [1883]. *Games and Songs of American Children*. Rev. ed. New York: Dover.

Olmsted, A. D. 1988. "Morally Controversial Leisure: The Social World of Gun Collectors." *Symbolic Interaction* 11 (2): 277–87. http://dx.doi.org/10.1525/ si.1988.11.2.277.

Opie, I., and P. Opie. 1959. *The Lore and Language of Schoolchildren*. Oxford: Clarendon Press.

Opie, I., and P. Opie. 1969. *Children's Games in Street and Playground*. Oxford: Clarendon Press.

Pellegrini, Ann. 2007. "Signaling through the Flames: Hell House Performance and Structures of Religious Feeling." *American Quarterly* 59 (3): 911–35. http://dx.doi. org/10.1353/aq.2007.0067.

Perkins, H. Wesley. 2002. "Social Norms and the Prevention of Alcohol Misuse in Collegiate Contexts." *Journal of Studies on Alcohol*, Supplement no. 14: 164–72. **Medline:12022722.**

Pettit, Thomas. 1997. "Folk Drama." In *Folklore: An Encyclopedia of Beliefs, Customs, Tales, Music, and Art*, ed. Thomas A. Green, 227–34. Santa Barbara, CA: ABC-CLIO.

Piaget, Jean. 1962. *Play, Dreams and Imitation in Childhood*. New York: Norton.

Ponton, Lynn. 1997. *The Romance of Risk: Why Teenagers Do the Things They Do*. New York: Basic Books.

Pope, Clementina. 2000. "The Horrors of Drinking and Driving." *The Montgomery Gazette*, 19 April.

Portner, Jessica. 1998. "Crisis Drills Make the Rounds, but Some Call It Overreaction." *Education Week* 18 (1): 1.

PR Newswire. 2001. "Judges Take Aim at Leading Cause of Death for American Youth; Courage to Live Program Takes DUI Courtroom to the Classroom." 1 October. http://www.judges.org.

Rabow, J., J. Stein, and T. Conley. 1999. "Teaching Social Justice and Encountering Society: The Pink Triangle Experiment." *Youth & Society* 30 (4): 483–514. http://dx.doi.org/10.1177/0044118X99030004005.

Rasmussen, Susan J. 1997. "Between Ritual, Theater, and Play: Blacksmith Praise at Tuareg Marriage." *Journal of American Folklore* 110 (435): 3–27. http://dx.doi.org/10.2307/541583.

Ratliff, George. 2002a. *Hell House.* Independent documentary film, 85 min.

Ratliff, George. 2002b. "Interview by Steve Inskeep." *National Public Radio Weekend Edition,* 17 August.

Reber, Craig. 2001. "School Event Becomes a Matter of Life, 'Death.'" *Dubuque Telegraph Herald,* 25 October.

Reed, Bracken. 2007. "The Best Plan for the Worst Case Scenarios." *Northwest Education* 13 (1): 31–6.

Reutter, Harold. 2000. "Mock Accident, Serious Lesson." *The Grand Island Independent,* 19 April.

Rickard, J. 1999. "'The Spectacle of Excess': The Emergence of Modern Professional Wrestling in the United States and Australia." *Journal of Popular Culture* 33 (1): 129–37. http://dx.doi.org/10.1111/j.0022-3840.1999.3301_129.x. Medline:21991649.

Roberts, John M., Malcolm J. Arth, and Robert R. Bush. 1959. "Games in Culture." *American Anthropologist* 61 (4): 597–605. http://dx.doi.org/10.1525/aa.1959.61.4.02a00050.

Rodriguez, Sylvia. 1996. *The Matachines Dance: Ritual Symbolism and Interethnic Relations in the Upper Rio Grande Valley.* Albuquerque: University of New Mexico Press.

Santino, Jack, ed. 2009. "The Ritualesque: Festival, Politics, and Popular Culture." *Western Folklore* 68 (1): 9–26.

Saunders, Terry McNeill. 1998. "Play, Performance and Professional Wrestling: An Examination of a Modern Day Spectacle of Absurdity." PhD diss., Program in Folklore and Mythology, University of California, Los Angeles.

Schechner, Richard. 1988. "Playing." *Play and Culture* 1 (1): 3–19.

Schechner, Richard. 1993. *The Future of Ritual.* London: Routledge. http://dx.doi.org/10.4324/9780203359150.

Schousboe, I. 1999. "Controversial Games and Their Implications." *Nordisk Psykologi* 51 (3): 175–91.

Scott, A. O. 2003. "Driver's Ed that Was Covered in Blood." *The New York Times,* 27 June.

Shaw, Robert A., Michael J. Rosati, Philip Salzman, Carol R. Coles, and Catherine McGeary. 1997. "Effects on Adolescent ATOD Behaviors and Attitudes of a Five-Year Community Partnership." *Evaluation and Program Planning* 20 (3): 307–13.

Shea, Rich. 2002. "Acting on Impulse." *Education Week* 13 (March): 22.

Shope, J. T., L. J. Molnar, and F. M. Streff. 1996. *Community-Wide Youth Impaired Driving Programs: Findings from Student Surveys in 1994 and 1996.* Ann Arbor: University of Michigan Transportation Research Institute.

Silverman, Ben. 2007. "Controversial Games." *Yahoo Games,* 17 September. http://video-games.yahoo.com/feature/controversial-games/530593-2.

Spradley, James P. 1979. *The Ethnographic Interview.* New York: Harcourt Brace.

Squires, Chase. 1998. "Church Houses Its Version of Hell." *St. Petersburg Times*, 31 October.

Stahl, Sandra. 1989. *Literary Folkloristics and the Personal Narrative*. Bloomington: Indiana University Press.

Steinhauer, Jennifer. 2009. "Scouts Train to Fight Terrorists, and More." *The New York Times*, 13 May.

Stryker, Jeff. 1999. "The Right Dose of Scare Tactics?" *The New York Times*, 31 October.

Suchman, Lucy A. 1987. *Plans and Situated Actions*. Cambridge: Cambridge University Press.

Sutton-Smith, Brian. 1979. "Epilogue: Play as Performance." In *Play and Learning*, ed. Brian Sutton-Smith, 295–322. New York: Gardner.

Sutton-Smith, Brian. 1997. *The Ambiguity of Play*. Cambridge, MA: Harvard University Press.

Sutton-Smith, Brian, and Diana Kelly-Byrne, eds. 1984. *The Masks of Play*. New York: Leisure Press.

Taft, Michael. 1996. "Folk Drama." In *American Folklore: An Encyclopedia*, ed. Jan Harold Brunvand, 208–10. New York: Garland Publishing.

Thigpen, Kenneth A., Jr. 1971. "Adolescent Legends in Brown County: A Survey." *Indiana Folklore* 4: 141–215.

Thompson, Stith. 1965. "The Star Husband Tale." In *The Study of Folklore*, ed. Alan Dundes, 414–74. Englewood Cliffs, NJ: Prentice-Hall. (Originally published in 1953 in *Studia Septentrionalia* 4: 93–163.)

Thyregod, Søren Tvermose. 1931. *Danmarks Sanglege*. Copenhagen: Det Schønbergske Forlag.

Turner, Victor. 1983. "Body, Brain, and Culture." *Zygon* 18 (3): 221–45. http://dx.doi.org/10.1111/j.1467-9744.1983.tb00512.x.

Twain, Mark. 1876. *The Adventures of Tom Sawyer*. Hartford, CT: American Publishing.

Varenne, Herve, and Ray McDermott. 1998. *Successful Failure: The School America Builds*. Boulder, CO: Westview.

Verhovek, Sam Howe. 1996. "Halloween Devils: Using Ghouls to Get to God." *The New York Times*, 27 October.

Von Sydow, Carl W. 1965. "Folktale Studies and Philology: Some Points of View." In *The Study of Folklore*, ed. Alan Dundes, 219–242. Englewood Cliffs, NJ: Prentice Hall.

Wood, Bret. 2003. *Hell's Highway: The True Story of Highway Safety Films*. A Livin' Man Production. Produced by Tommy Gibbons and Bret Wood. Directed by Bret Wood. 90 min.

Woodman, E. C. 1994. "Patterns of Participation in Alcohol and Other Drug Education/Prevention Programs among Students in Grades Six through Twelve." *Dissertation Abstracts International* 55 (1): 49-A–50-A.

Index

Abrahams, Roger, 60, 109, 110
Abundant Life Christian Center (Colo.), 27
accidents. *See* mock accidents
administrators, 71, 75–76, 84, 97, 86
adolescents. *See* teenagers
adults: behavior of, 90–91, 93; collaboration, 86–87; at mock accidents, 69–70; on student reactions, 88–89, 112. *See also* parents
Adventures of Tom Sawyer, The (Twain), 48, 79, 100, 127 agency, play and, 50–51
Alabama, Judgement House pageant, 28
alcohol abuse: in adolescents, 20–21; high school education, 29–30
Alcohol and Alcohol Problems Science Database, 20
American Top 40, 33
Anastas, Robert, 19
anti-drug programs, 21
Arratia, Maria-Inés, 115
Arvada (Colo.), Hell House in, 27
assemblies, 85; E15M, 39–40, 92–93; framing at, 72–73; Living Dead at, 76–77; memorialization in, 106–7
attention seeking/getting, 101, 102, 104–5; media and, 118–19
audiences, 83; in folk drama, 7–8; mock accident, 51–52; play framing in, 72–73

BAC. *See* blood alcohol concentration
Bang Bang You're Dead (play), 30, 115
Bateson, Gregory, 61, 62, 73, 133; "A Theory of Play and Fantasy," 48
Bauman, Richard, 50
beauty pageants, 103–4
behaviors, 21; of adults, 90–91; during E15M program, 91–92; social norms of, 19–20
beliefs, YouTube documentation of, 120–21
Beresin, Anna Richman, 103, 115–16
Best, Joel, *Damned Lies and Statistics,* 43
Beyond Scared Straight (TV show), 26
blood alcohol concentration (BAC), 16, 17

border violence, simulations of, 114
Bordin, Judy, 43, 44
boundaries, play framing, 51, 56–57
Boy Scouts of America, law-enforcement camps, 114–15
Bucks County (Penn.), terrorism camp, 114
bull fighting, as dark play, 115
Bully (video game), 113

California, 22; drunk-driving deaths in, 40–41; E15M programs in, 6, 11, 31–32, 36, 71–72, 89, 93–95, 98, 102, 105, 106; E15M websites, 34–35; hoaxes, 85–86; law-enforcement camps, 114–15
California Alcoholic Beverage Control Grant Assistance to Law Enforcement (GALE), 32
California Department of Alcoholic Beverage Control, 89, 103; surveys, 43–44
California State University, Chico, Child Development Program, 43
Carroll, Jon, 86
CDC. *See* Centers for Disease Control
Cedar Hill (Tex.), Hell House in, 27
Cemeteries, in E15M programs, 37–38
Centers for Disease Control (CDC), on alcohol-related crashes, 15, 16
Cerritos (Calif.), E15M program, 32
chaperones, at Living Dead retreats, 75–76
Chico (Calif.), E15M program in, 31–32, 130
churches, morality plays, 26–27
Clark County (Wash.), 115
collaboration, 5, 93–94; in folk drama, 7–8
colleges, 19, 35
Colorado, 26, 27, 131–32
Columbine High School shootings, 40; role-playing games on, 113–14
community, 5; collaboration and cooperation of, 94–95
community festivals, 56
computer games, role-playing, 112–13
contracts, 22

143